THE HOLLIES SCHOOL

—— LIGHT OAKS ——

Childhood Memories of People and Special Places

Dorothy M. Norris

ISBN 0-9548253-0-6

Printed by Brookes Design to Print, Sneyd Street,
Sneyd Green, Stoke-on-Trent ST6 2NP

THE HOLLIES SCHOOL

LIGHT OAKS

Childhood Memories of People and Special Places

Published by
Bramble Publications
32 Red Lane, Meltham, Holmfirth
Yorkshire HD9 5LG Tel: 01484 851976

ISBN 0-9548253-0-6

Written and edited by Dorothy M. Norris 2003

Printed by Brookes Design to Print, Sneyd Street,
Sneyd Green, Stoke-on-Trent ST6 2NP

Rev. Arthur Bird and Annis, the founders of the Hollies School.

ACKNOWLEDGEMENTS

People have contributed their childhood memories to this history of a small private school in North Staffordshire. I have received numerous telephone calls and letters expressing interest, enquiries that often resulted in further correspondence and the development of new friendships. One individual who responded soon after I began my initial search was Mary Bartlam. Her interest and enthusiasm in tracing former pupils was very encouraging and I would like to express my thanks for this early assistance.

I am grateful indeed to those who have contributed in some way to the following pages: Jeanie Gray, Joyce Grindey, David Heath, June Holford, Marjorie Hollowood, Iris Johnson, Alma Mifflin, Maureen Leese, Joan Millington, Sylvia Pierpoint, Daphne Ratcliffe, Rosemary Robson, Peter Sherratt, Jeanne Townend, Valerie Whittaker, Catherine and Elizabeth Wood.

I am very appreciative, too, for the lengthier submissions from Edward Bottomley, Michael Brookes, Christine Clipson, Jeremy Francis, Bill Hassall, Sylvia Myatt and Heather Nicholson. These have been included where possible in their entirety. A deep thank you to you all. Special thanks, in addition, for those who have provided photographs, Christine Clipson, Joan Millington, Sylvia Myatt, and my daughter Ruth Francis.

I have had much encouragement from friends and family, both here and overseas and wish to thank Tony Mason and Valerie McGloughlin, for their comments and suggestions after reading the manuscript. More happily engaged when using a typewriter, my daughter Heather's assistance in helping me to overcome my fear of a computer was invaluable and I am very grateful for her help when things went wrong.

Finally, I am particularly grateful to my son Jeremy for his suggestions and advice, and deeply appreciative of the time he has spent on preparing the index and ensuring the successful completion of the project.

PREFACE

Some years ago when I was living on Vancouver Island, British Columbia, I met a couple who had emigrated in the 1950s from Stoke-on-Trent. The husband recognised my accent, and over a cup of tea we discovered how much we all had in common. The White Hart café, Duncan, was an unlikely setting to be reminiscing about our childhood days in North Staffordshire. Geraldine Chester (nee Scott) and I had both attended the Orme Girls' School at Newcastle-under-Lyme. Reginald, her husband, had lived in Hartshill as a child, not far from where my Grandmother, Annis Bird, had started a private school in 1915. The Hollies, as the school would soon become known, was relocated in the late 1920s to Baddeley Edge and then to Light Oaks. There I received my own primary education, growing up in the family home beside the school. The Chesters also had some link with that area, a strange coincidence when we were all so far from 'home'!

Like all children, I had taken my home for granted, and had given little thought to either how the school started or its later history. I first began to realise how little I knew about it when I was contacted by another former pupil of both The Hollies and the Orme Girls who was living in British Columbia. Jeanie Gray (nee Lawrie) wanted to know more about the place that had left her with such happy memories, and asked questions I could not immediately answer. My own childhood memories had been recorded already but they were a very small part of the fifty-three years during which the various principals of the Hollies pursued their largely philanthropic roles.

Gathering material has proved a journey of discovery. It has required some detective work, made possible by research into family papers and the interest of former pupils who have contributed in many different ways to this book. Many people contacted me following the publicity provided by the Stoke-on-Trent Evening Sentinel and I am deeply grateful to them all. The Hollies Private School together with the family home, occupied an unique position in the village of Light Oaks, not only as a place of learning but as a rendezvous for groups of many ages, air-raid wardens, evacuees, youth hostellers, and boys from Smallthorne Junior School. The local branch of the Church of England Men's Society and a Bible class had their meetings in the house. Throughout the years the two buildings opened their doors to a succession of peoples from the surrounding countryside. I have included a few of the local names that I remember from my own childhood and hope that others will share the pleasure I discovered in recording these historic memories.

CONTENTS

INDEX OF PLATES

CHAPTER 1

My grandfather was born in 1857, almost one and a half centuries ago, a distinction he shared with Robert Baden Powell, Edward Elgar and Joseph Conrad among others. Queen Victoria was in the twentieth year of her reign. England's Royal Navy was engaged in the destruction of the Chinese fleet, and the Indian mutiny against British rule took place. The family had strong links with both the navy and the army but it is unlikely that these events would have had any effect on the young Arthur Herbert Bird.

He was one of at least nine children, few of whom reached maturity despite a caring and comfortable home. It is more probable, judging by the man he would become, that his adolescence was influenced by the many scientific discoveries of the period and the ongoing controversy over Darwin's 'On the Origin of Species' and subsequent publications. The eruption of the Krakatoa volcano occurred when he was twenty-six, and his many landscape paintings with their spectacular sunsets indicate that he joined the wave of sky painting that became the current rage among the artists of his day. He spent some time at Trinity College, Dublin, liberal in his interests that embraced both science and the classics. Years later he confided to his older son and daughter that at one time he had considered a career in medicine. He seems to have continued with his studies for some time. In 1881 he wrote and published a book that he dedicated to two sisters. In his early thirties he married a lady from Bradford. Annis was very devout and extremely persuasive. She could have influenced his eventual choice of career for at the age of thirty-four he became a deacon, and two years later was ordained by the Bishop of Ripon, the same year that their first child was born.

He started his ministry in the Parish of Great Smeaton as curate of St. Mary's, Appleton Wiske. It was a comfortable Living, but his wife Annis was something of a crusader and managed to persuade him that they should be working among the poor. So they left the fields and flowering hedgerows for the smoke laden skies of the Potteries. It was 1894. He was thirty-seven, Annis was twenty-nine, and their son Francis not yet two.

11

During the next eight years he was licensed to Holy Trinity, St Luke's and Wellington Parish Church, Hanley, before the Bishop of Lichfield granted him the position of 'Stipendiary Curate in the Parish churches of Bucknall and Bagnall, at a yearly stipend of £150 to be paid quarterly'. He and Annis would have four more children, but they lost their youngest son Oswald to Diphtheria. They had to move twice due to house fires, but subsequent moves to more desirable properties indicate that Arthur had some private income. In September 1904, he was licensed to the office of Chaplain to the Stoke-on-Trent Union Workhouse. The family moved to 'Hazelmere', Queen's Road, Hartshill, a property more suited to the needs of his family.

Annis Bird, my grandmother, led a busy life. She visited the sick and needy, supervised several servants and a stableman, and provided the early education for her children. She was devoted to her husband, and frequently concerned about him, as he was not a strong man. She invariably put his comfort and needs before her own and those of her children, often suppressing their boisterous behaviour in case he was disturbed.

Before her marriage, Annis had served several years as a pupil teacher at Whetley Lane Board School, Bradford. She had a certificate in Animal Physiology and elementary and intermediate certificates issued by the Tonic Sol-fa College. She and Arthur played the flute, mandolin and the piano, so their children must have experienced many musical evenings during their childhood and adolescence. Annis, like many a Victorian wife, seems to have remained in the background. She left nothing material of her own life for her descendants. In sharp contrast, Arthur had a vast library and was an inveterate collector of curios and entomological specimens. A large cabinet housed medical, zoological and botanical slides, and he spent much time at his microscope. He continued to paint, mainly in oils, and was a keen photographer and model railway enthusiast. His steam train pulled its rolling stock on three inch gauge rails around their large garden. No doubt, Annis and her daughters quietly watched while the boys shared their father's hobby. In the early years of their marriage, Arthur had enjoyed carpentry, constructing heavy pieces of oak furniture for their home that he embellished with intricate carvings of leaves and flowers. Annis must have supervised the servants who did the dusting and polishing, a job my mother undertook in my childhood until the family realised how impracticable the heavy furniture was in the smaller rooms of a 1930s home.

Annis read through Arthur's carefully prepared sermons and filed them away while he made notes in Latin and Greek. As a family, they played croquet on fine summer evenings, but in the winter, she would sew or knit while the older members of the family enjoyed billiards, or watched their father's slides with the gas lit magic lantern. They all enjoyed amateur theatricals in the privacy of the home.

In 1906, Annis decided to return to teaching. Her four surviving children were at this time fourteen, eleven, seven and four so someone must have been employed to look after the little ones. For the next six years she was in charge of needlework at Newchapel Church of England School, travelling to and fro by pony and trap. She had taught both her daughters to sew, insisting on a high standard of workmanship.

Why she returned to teaching at this period of their marriage is unknown. It is obvious that Arthur supported her decision. His own duties at the Workhouse possibly kept him away from home for much of the day. She found teaching deeply satisfying, and no doubt regretted resigning in 1912, a year of public unrest. There was the London Dock strike, the Transport Workers' strike and the British Coal Workers' strike. Perhaps it was the latter that caused Arthur and Annis to decide that her daily journey to school through a predominately coal mining area was no longer safe. She would not have made any such decision on her own.

Throughout 1913, relations were tense between France and Germany, and the following year Germany declared war on both Russia and France and invaded Belgium. Soon one of Annis's nephews in Bradford was working with a group of Belgian refugees while his sister and a small group of friends were busy fund-raising on their behalf. They performed operettas, bold behaviour for genteel young ladies following the suffragist demonstrations in London the previous year. There were close links between the two families so it is not surprising that some months later Arthur and Annis offered a home to two of the refugees. These young ladies would share the family life for several years and were later remembered with much affection.

Francis Bird, my Uncle, had attended Newcastle High School from 1904 to 1912 and was in the school cadet Officer Training Corps for four years. He was awarded a first class certificate in Musketry before he left to go to Dublin University. Following in his father's footsteps, he entered Trinity, passing exams in Euclid, Trigonometry, Algebra, Greek and Latin. The following year he passed Mechanics and Logic. World War I was gathering momentum and one European country after another was declaring war on its neighbours. Francis left University, his studies incomplete. In such uncertain times he may have wished to be nearer home and to start contributing to the family income. His sisters were attending the Orme Girls' School but Phyllis, the eldest, was about to continue her studies in Dublin, too. His younger brother, Lionel, was at Newcastle High School.

Francis commenced teaching at Smallthorne Council Junior Boys. In his spare time, he trained for the St John Ambulance award 'to give first aid to the injured'. Then in November 1915, he volunteered for the Royal Navy. His Naval records list him as a School Teacher and show that he served on three ships, 'Vivid', 'Macedonia', and another vessel, the name unfortunately faded and undecipherable. He had a further course of duty on 'Vivid' before he returned to civilian life in 1919. Working as a Sick Bay attendant, he experienced the traumatic aftermaths of naval warfare. He narrowly missed drowning off Cape Town, and later saw further action in South American waters.

 His father was now in his sixties and in poor health. Francis took on the duties of head of the household though Arthur had the final word when a decision had to be made. This situation may have been partly responsible for a personal tragedy to which Francis never referred and his sisters kept secret throughout his life. In later years, they said it was too long ago to discuss. This loyalty to each other about their private affairs has left many tantalising gaps in their individual stories.

My generation believed that Francis was a bachelor. In fact, he had been married but his wife deserted him, severing her connection with the family. Marriage was considered sacrosanct, so a divorce was out of the question as far as his parents were concerned. His own views are unknown, but had it been possible he would have married again. He had a great affection for another young lady whose premature death affected him deeply. Nora Swift's portrait hung in his room. Many years later, his sisters would place it and the letters the young couple had exchanged beside him in his coffin.

Phyllis, Arthur and Annis's second child had been a very small and weakly premature baby so her survival in 1895 was remarkable. Her parents considered her as special, and were very proud of her academic achievements. After she passed the first Dublin exams, her ambition was to gain a degree in botany. Then came the first Zeppelin attack on London and a German airship bombed the east coast. The blockade of England had begun. There were submarine attacks and many merchant ships were being destroyed. Her father feared for her safety and after a very brief period at University she was called home. Phyllis was a dutiful daughter but she was very disappointed that her studies had to be abandoned. She returned to further sad news. One of their close childhood friends had been killed in action, the young man whom her parents had considered an eligible suitor for her though perhaps her feelings were not so serious. No doubt, she would have accepted their choice. She did not stay at home but accepted an invitation to Chatsworth where she worked briefly as a governess. Here she did fall deeply in love, but with someone, her parents deemed unsuitable. Possibly the Unknown worked on the estate! Again, she was summoned home. Her brief period of independence was over.

Phyllis now turned to agriculture, perhaps the closest she could be to her lost love. She became a keen gardener, grew vegetables, kept chickens and began breeding goats. Food was increasingly in short supply so her help was invaluable. Casualties among her brother's former school friends were high, though now she had no desire to marry any of the possible survivors. She was unaware that her mother was already planning her future.

Jeanie, my mother, was the fourth child of the family. A brother Oswald had been born in 1897 followed by Jeanie in 1899. Oswald's early death from diphtheria must have been incomprehensible to the little girl when she lost her playmate. How she and the other children escaped infection is unknown. Jeanie was a very private person who in later years revealed little of her childhood, teenage dreams and aspirations. She had accompanied her father on one occasion to the Workhouse, a visit she never forgot. She went with her mother to Newchapel for a brief visit, too, but was not allowed to enter the school for fear of contracting some disease. She recalled sitting in the pony and trap for what seemed a long time, feeling lonely. She visited the sick and elderly of the parish with her mother, and as soon as she was old enough helped to organise her father's papers and to deal with household matters.

Jeanie enjoyed serious reading, needlework and sketching. During her early teens, she entered and won a National competition sponsored by Arthur Mee, Editor of the Children's Encyclopedia. Photographs show her in their Hartshill garden in the ankle length dresses of the period, a large hat shading her serene face, and the family Great Dane at her side.

She left school just after her sixteenth birthday in 1915, her education deemed of less importance than her sister's, and her future role in the household apparently determined by her parents. Their plans for her future, however good their motive, ignored the needs of their youngest daughter who had a lively enquiring mind, was an avid reader and regularly corresponded with cousins who had achieved various degrees of independence. She was an obedient loving daughter, but they failed to see that she might want more of life than they had planned for her immediate future.

In September 1915, Annis turned two of the rooms at 'Hazelmere', Queen's Road, Hartshill, into schoolrooms. It appears to have been a sudden decision, but she may have had a long-term plan and realised the current circumstances were ideal to start their own school. The earliest entries in the now tattered and crumbling admittance register show that the first pupils were boarders. Their home addresses were so close that it is likely that only some incident of World War I could have led to their staying with the family. Annis may have anticipated the demand for a short-term boarding facility when there were so many domestic crises in the neighbourhood, and saw a means of providing useful occupations for both her daughters. Phyllis's academic qualifications would make her a suitable joint Principal, and Jeanie would make an ideal housekeeper and surrogate mother to little boarders. Annis will have discussed the details with her husband, but it is unlikely that her daughters were advised until the plan was agreed.

She arranged the teaching between herself and Phyllis. French lessons were provided by one of the Belgian ladies. Arthur conducted the morning prayers though soon he would be fully occupied in ministering to the wounded in Stoke Military Hospital. Annis taught the younger pupils, but carried out all instruction in Scripture, Needlework and Music for which she was well qualified.

The new school was in great demand and numbers increased annually. Among the first pupils were a Joan Jervis, Basil Seddon, Marjorie Hughes, and siblings Nora, Edna and Eric Swift. The school functioned more as an extended family than a business, and fees seem to have been arranged on an individual basis. The Birds were all singularly unbusiness like and would remain so. Annis's priorities were to provide a sound education and strong religious values. She had no salaries to consider, as her helpers were all within the family. Presumably Phyllis and Jeanie had a small allowance from their father for their personal needs and the Belgian ladies had free board and lodging although they may have had some private income. Any surplus money Annis received was put back into the school. Phyllis made the first school desks, probably with her father's guidance, but the household furniture, the family books and other useful possessions were put to general use.

With the cessation of hostilities and the safe return of their eldest son the family moved to more suitable premises, and the 'Hollies', a private residence in Princess Road, Hartshill, became the Hollies Private School.

It was the family home, also, but perhaps Jeanie found it hardest to adjust. Francis had resumed his teaching career at Smallthorne but remained the support and confident of his sisters and younger brother who was now pursuing his own career in the Merchant Navy. Francis always found time to listen, offer advice and help when required, a role he would maintain throughout his life. Their parents had each other, and Phyllis, outside the classroom, had her garden, goats and poultry. Jeanie was left to supervise the large household. She cared for the boarders, repaired clothing, and dealt with an hundred and one domestic duties. It was a demanding life for a young woman. Her paint box remained closed, and her charming sketches came to an abrupt end.

As in the war years, the school continued to provide a social need, taking in a number of children for relatively short periods. One can only guess at the traumas in their backgrounds, but the Hollies provided a loving and safe environment for as long as it was required, a policy that would never change.

Plate 1   *The Hollies School*

Scenes from vicarage life 1900 - 1917.

Plate 2. The Hollies Private School, Hartshill in the 1920s.

Plate 3 *The Hollies School*

Newchapel Church School 1911.

Rev. Bird with administrative and nursing staff in front of the Stoke-on-Trent Union Workhouse School used in 1914 -1918 as a Military Hospital.

Father and son,
Arthur and Francis Bird (1915)

Plate 5 *The Hollies School*

Phyllis, 1914 (left), and Jeanie Bird, 1920s (above)

Boarders at the Hollies, Hartshill.

Sydney Arnold and Frank Brown prior to their arrival in England.

Annis with Nora Brown and Phyllis with Jean Elliot.

Prospect House, Baddeley Edge and the Chapel, Fowlers Lane as they appear today.

Plate 7   *The Hollies School*

The Hollies School Light Oakes (1934) including (Back row) Phyllis Bird, Jean Elliot, Mary Lyth, (Second row) Peter Phillips, (Front row) John Phillips, John Wood, Dorothy Brown and Frank Bradley.

CHAPTER 2

During the early years of Arthur Bird's ministry in Stoke-on-Trent, he had recognised a photograph of one of his wife's relatives in the home of a parishioner. This strange coincidence led to a visit from one of Annis's cousins. Sydney Brown was only eight years her junior and consequently seemed old to her children. He had been wounded in the Boer war and having emigrated to Canada in 1906 he seemed a somewhat romantic figure to his young cousins. In 1921, he visited them again, this time with two young sons, and arranged to leave them as boarders at the Hollies Private School. The little boys, Sydney Arnold and Frank were six and four at the time. They were two very troubled children due to some recent experiences, Frank particularly bewildered by what had happened in his life. Years later Sydney Arnold recalled that Jeanie had been a real mother to them at a time when they were desperate for love and security. He remembered her bandaging knees after falls and reading them bedtime stories, sitting beside Frank until he had fallen asleep and comforting him when he had nightmares. No doubt, she was fulfiling her usual role with the little boarders.

As the months went by Annis was troubled. The whole family knew that Jeanie had a great affection and admiration for the older Sydney, dating from their first meeting when she was a little girl. When he returned to collect his sons he told them that he had obtained a divorce from his wife in Alberta. Annis and Arthur were appalled. Although 3747 divorces had been granted in England the previous year they were still considered a scandal, and no doubt Sydney would have been asked to leave immediately if it had not been for the presence of his sons. As it was, for a short time he stayed on, observing and being observed. He was a man of some charm, both interesting and clever, and a welcome guest for the younger members of the family.

One day he took Jeanie and the boys to Rudyard Lake for the day and unfortunately, they missed the last train. As far as he was concerned, it was unfortunate but easily remedied. He booked separate rooms at an inn for himself and the boys, and his innocent young cousin, and probably gave the matter apart from the inconvenience little thought. Jeanie was still almost a child to the tough old soldier, twenty-six years her senior. It was only on their return home on the first available train the following day that he realised the enormity of his behaviour. No doubt, he tried to laugh it off. He had done nothing wrong. Arthur was furious. Jeanie, the main recipient of his wrath was totally unaware of why her father was so angry and her mother so distraught. It had been quite an exciting adventure for her and one she had been looking forward to relating to Francis and Phyllis. Now she heard that she had disgraced the family. Furthermore, her father said 'you are no more a daughter of mine', something she must have received with a flood of tears. Poor innocent Jeanie, ignorant of the facts of life as were all the young ladies of her age, and which even then Annis failed to explain. Such matters were not a subject for conversation. In the tirade that followed Arthur told Sydney that he and his sons were no longer welcome and they left, but not before Sydney had secretly proposed marriage to Jeanie and devised a plan. Francis must have been party to their secret for Jeanie left, too, going to live with some cousins in Bradford until Sydney could arrange for their Civil wedding in Liverpool where he had a married sister. Arthur would always consider this ceremony invalid but the views of Annis at the time are unknown. She would always condemn divorce but the circumstances in which she had lost a daughter caused her much sadness, and possibly for the first time it was a grief she could not share with Arthur. The day after the wedding Sydney, Jeanie and her two stepsons sailed for South Africa.

One can only guess at the chaos that followed Jeanie's sudden departure from the Hollies. More domestic staff had to be employed and supervised, and Annis and Phyllis must have worked very long hours. Realisation of the amount of work Jeanie had done may have caused her parents some soul searching, but even so they were slow to forgive her. Whatever explanations were given to parents and children for her sudden departure were inadequate. A former pupil told me that it had been a great mystery at the time. Perhaps Annis secretly admitted to herself that the situation could have been better handled.

Jeanie's letters to Francis would soon cause him concern for she advised that their stay in South Africa would be short. The work Sydney had envisaged had not materialised. He was a surveyor and cartographer. He decided that they should continue on to Australia, a long sea voyage in those days that became even longer when Sydney's search for work took them north up the coast to Queensland. Jeanie was by now regretting her impetuous marriage. Life in the Australian bush with a tough ex-soldier old enough to be her father, no near neighbours and two disturbed and often rebellious stepsons was far removed from the security of home. When the arrival of her first child some two years later was imminent, she could no longer cope with the rigorous life they led. Francis financed her voyage back to England. She did not return home immediately and after she gave birth to a daughter stayed in Liverpool with Sydney's sister. The reconciliation with her parents some considerable time later was probably due to family diplomacy and their desire to see their first grandchild. Once they agreed she could return to Hartshill Jeanie soon resumed her former role, managing the needs of the Hollies School and the household. It was a responsible task with little reward, but she was glad to be home.

Five pupils who attended the Hollies Private School throughout this period were the Bills family of Hartshill. They were Norah, Godfrey, Eileen, Eva and Thomas Bills. Eva and her older siblings started school at 'Hazelmere' prior to the move to Princes Road. She was not quite four years old, and remembers calling Annis and Arthur Mamma and Dadda Bird. Her memory of Annis was happy and linked with music, and of Phyllis seated at the piano. "She was not very good"' Eva told me, but Phyllis never went willingly to the keyboard. Jeanie was always called Miss Jeanie. One of the boarders in her charge was a girl called Joyce who was Eva's friend. Eva would spend eleven years at the Hollies.

Marjorie Hollowood (nee Lawrie) attended the school from 1923, the year of Jeanie's return to England, to 1927.

"I got to know the family well", she recalled. "Mrs. Bird was of medium height and wore attractive navy woollen cardigans over ankle length skirts. Miss Bird was more ascetic looking. The Rev. Bird wore a clerical 'soup plate' hat. 'The Hollies' or 'The Birds' as we children called the school was in a good-sized house in Princes Road. We lived in the same road. When I was four years old and able to read, I was considered old enough to go to The Hollies. I already knew that the smaller children were taught upstairs by Mrs Bird, the older ones downstairs by Miss Bird. On my first day I was surprised to be taken upstairs and announced that I wished to be downstairs with the big ones. Very kindly and tactfully, Mrs Bird told my parents that I was not quite ready for school. In a few months, they tried again and I settled in this time. Mrs.

21

Bird was a born teacher and gifted at the work. I imagine that there were twenty-five children upstairs and the same number downstairs. The school was highly respected. I remember Miss Bird coming into the room one day with the post, saying a little ruefully, "as usual all ours have got in". She was referring to the Orme Girls School to which eventually my sister and I went. At seven and three-quarters, I was the youngest for my first year there, another tribute to the Birds' teaching. I was very happy at the Hollies. Mrs Bird would start off our day with a tuning-fork, sounding the note for a hymn. Quite often this would be *There's a friend for little children,* and as we sang I would gaze out of the window at the rooks busy in the high trees. The day started with mental arithmetic. It was like a game. We stood in a large circle. If you got the answer right you moved up a place and vice versa if wrong. Clever Beryl Sturgess was invariably in top place!" (Beryl was at The Hollies from 1925 to 1927.)

Marjorie remembers that in the early days the Rev. Bird would sometimes appear. "We were greatly indebted to him for the pattern bricks he made, flat geometric shapes coloured dusty pink, blue and green. They were kept in a large bottom drawer and children were allowed to play with them as a reward for good behaviour. I often had a go but I suspect it was to stop me fidgeting.

Playtime was in the garden near to the hen-run. Boys and girls played amicably together, often forming what we fondly called trams".

Marjorie says that when her mother who was also the daughter of a clergyman was seriously ill, she and her sister, another Jeanie, boarded at the Hollies. At that time, she was allowed to explore the 'treasures' in the attics. "I was especially interested in an antiquated magic lantern and sometimes dipped into a box of prize books!" she told me. "That interesting collection of objects seems to me now to reflect the Birds' erudite background."

Sylvia Pierpoint (nee Hodgskiss) spent a year at The Hollies from 1924 to 1925. Apparently, she had started school at St. Dominics. Her mother's aim was to get her into the Orme Girls' School but Sylvia failed the entrance examination. Her mother said that it was because she had got her clean socks dirty! So she was sent to the Hollies in Princes Road. Her earliest memory was of a boy called Arthur Spark, the doctor's son.

The Register shows that he was at the school from 1922 to 1926. "He was a naughty little boy", Sylvia recalled. (He was only six at the time!)

Sylvia told me that the whole school entered an Art examination, all age groups being taught together. They had to do a Still Life drawing of a sock. (Socks seem to have played an important role in her life!) Her drawing won a prize, a Wedgwood vase. They had a marvellous French teacher, too, whom she feels was responsible for the credit in French she later gained at the Orme, having passed the entrance exam after her year at the Hollies.

Jeanie Gray (nee Lawrie) was at the school from 1925 to 1929. Her memories of my mother Jeanie Brown are as follows: "She had a very pleasant face and manner, with a country-fresh complexion and seemed to be always in the background, presumably looking after things behind the scenes. As a child I was vaguely aware that her husband was overseas somewhere. My young mind visualised him as a big game hunter in darkest Africa. My memories of the Hollies are mainly of the classroom and particularly the coloured blocks we used on special occasions, and the garden where we played. It was possibly in 1925 when King George V and Queen Mary visited the Potteries and opened a wing of the North Staffs Royal Infirmary. The Hollies' pupils stood on benches to see over the wooden fence and waved little Union Jack flags as the royal entourage drove by".

"Some memories are not to my credit. My sister and I have laughed many a time over an incident that I am sure happened to me and she is equally positive it happened to her. Mrs. Bird was bending over a child's work in the seat next to mine, and I was tempted by the view of her knitted tweed posterior to give it a little pat. I really thought she would not feel it when I decided to pat a little harder. She turned around saying 'You are a very rude little girl. Hold out your hand'. Smack, smack! Marjorie insists it was she that did this terrible thing, so did BOTH of us have such a silly urge! Another incident I remember - I coveted the apple Aileen Scott always had in her lunch box. One day I took it and ate it. When Aileen said 'Oh, where is my apple?' the other children said 'Jeanie Lawrie took it. She never has an apple for lunch and today we saw her eating one'. "I am sure the children did not tell Mrs. Bird but they meted out their own brand of punishment when we left school and walked up Princes Road to go home. The children, maybe six of them, flogged me with knotted handkerchiefs all the way up the road. I was crying, and when a woman asked what they were doing they told her and she went on her way, probably thinking justice was being done!" (Aileen Scott was a pupil between 1926 and 1928.)

Jeanie added a further colourful and poignant memory of life at the Hollies. She writes, "I recall Lionel Bird dressing up with a sheet over his head, coming into the room with a pair of horns on top, which was frightening." (The youngest Bird was in his early twenties at the time, and probably on leave from the Merchant Navy The horns were those of a water buffalo mounted on a red velvet plaque which in my childhood was hung on the wall of the room we called the library.)

Jeanie refers to the time she and her sister boarded at the Hollies. "It was Christmas Eve and we woke up aware of something at the foot of the bed. On investigation, we found our Christmas Stockings full of interesting things, the most fun being the rolled up whistles with a feather on the end. How we blew, enjoying the noise we were making. Then someone came into the room, telling us what naughty children we were, and gathered up all our goodies. 'Now go to sleep', we were told."

My mother's comings and goings caused considerable speculation among the children although Jeanie Lawrie could not recall my father Sydney's unexpected return. Perhaps it occurred during a school holiday! After failing to persuade Jeanie to return to him in 1923 Sydney and his sons had gone back to Canada. In 1927, he revisited Hartshill. He was full of his old charm, and promised that if she would give him a second chance her life would be easier. He described the house he had bought for her and their little daughter Nora, and finally she agreed to return to Canada with him. This time the effect on the home and the school must have been catastrophic. No one person could replace her hours of dedicated unpaid work that had included the full-time care of another little girl the same age as Nora. Phyllis, with her parents' and Francis's support had collected the little Jean Elliot from a London Orphanage. Officially, Phyllis's foster child, the intention was that Jean would be a companion and sister for Nora. Now Nora was going to Canada.

At last, Jeanie's contribution to the smooth running of the Hollies was openly acknowledged by her mother, ailing father, and sister. Perhaps they tried to persuade her to stay. It seems likely but there is no way of knowing. She had always had Francis's support and he assured her before she left that if her new life did not work out as they all hoped he would arrange her return home once again.

Sydney had speculated in property for many years. The new house in Alberta he had described to Jeanie was seen by her but sold before they moved in. Perhaps he had not intended to mislead her but he could not resist a good offer. She was certainly unaware of what she would face in Alberta. One of the few things she ever mentioned about Canada was that he had shot wolves from the doorway of their home. She had been proud of the fact that he was a marksman and had been part of the Canadian team at Bisley on several occasions. When after a short period they moved to British Columbia he again did not prepare her for what lay ahead. She was unfitted for the rigors of pioneer life but seems to have shown remarkable stamina and courage. Tracing my mother's steps half a century later, my half brothers threw some light on what had occurred prior to my birth. Sydney could be very violent with his sons, particularly when suffering recurrent pain from his Boer war injuries. These were aggravated without a doubt by the Canadian climate. After experiencing his anger on numerous occasions, Jeanie became afraid to interfere, particularly when she again found herself pregnant. The teenage boys fled repeatedly to the forest and mountains to escape his black moods and she was blamed for not controlling them better. She must have been very aware of the dangers of the Back Country with its bears, wolves, and cheetahs. There was the even greater risk of the boys getting lost and dying of exposure, but she was powerless to control her tough stepsons.

After I was born the fears she must have expressed in letters home prompted Francis to again arrange for her return to England. Sydney accepted her decision to leave, but never lost hope that one day she would return to him. Divorce was never considered by either of them. She seldom referred to her former life in Australia, and refused to talk about Canada, a topic of considerable interest to myself as I was Canadian, a fact my Uncle Francis encouraged me to remember. Perhaps my mother's hurts ran too deep!

She soon resumed her role as homemaker for her mother, elder brother, sister, and now three small children. Her father had died during her last absence, and the family circumstances had changed, too, in those years of the Great Depression. She appears to have been unaware that they no longer occupied the spacious Hartshill property. The move may have taken place after we left Vancouver Island on the long journey home. This time she would find very different circumstances from those she had left with such anticipation for the future.

Chapter 3

My memory of my new home was of a somewhat frightening place. Our arrival at Baddeley Edge after the long and arduous trip across Canada, followed by an extremely rough Atlantic voyage on the Cunard steamship Mauretania, probably left our small family in a very fragile state. On the train journey from Vancouver to Montreal my sister had been bewildered and distressed. I had been left in the care of a supportive black car attendant for much of the time. The sea voyage was one of enormous waves and breakages, not that we had anything to break. Judging by the absence of any Canadian memorabilia in my childhood, we had travelled extremely light.

'Prospect House' had been built on a rocky outcrop, and was known as 'Gilman's Folly' to the people of Baddeley Green and Stockton Brook in the valley below. Gilman was the builder, I was told by Elizabeth Wood, who had been a pupil at the relocated Hollies School housed in rented premises not far away. The house, a red brick and white stucco building was totally exposed to the elements and seemed to tower above the little stone cottages dotting the hillside below. On a clear day it could be seen from many miles away, something I found very reassuring when I began to associate it with home. The steep hillside was a problem to all but our free-range hens that flourished on the rocky incline. I lost a wooden hoop down the slope on one occasion and never got it back.

Inside, the house was very dark. The windows were small and the rooms dim. The black cast iron kitchen range seemed to occupy the greater part of our kitchen living room. There was a huge iron kettle that stood on a circular hob. It swung around over the coals to bring water to the boil. A bread oven flanked the side of the open fire, the coals contained by several horizontal iron bars. Occasionally cinders would work their way through, particularly when the fire was stirred into life with a great long poker, and they would lie smouldering on the stone-flagged hearth until their heat was spent. The stairs to the bedrooms and attics were steep and narrow. Candlesticks stood beside each bed and the candles cast grotesque flickering shadows on the walls. Downstairs there were beautiful brass table lamps. They gave a warm and welcoming light. Cleaning the soot from their glass chimneys was one of the many daily tasks my mother took for granted.

The nearest bus stop was some distance away, down a steep and windswept lane. The banks and dry stonewalls offered little protection from the fierce gusts of wind that blew from the surrounding moorland. That first winter a blizzard cut off all amenities in the area for several weeks. Snow drifted higher than the rooftops of the nearest cottages, and tunnels had to be dug to the doors so that milk, eggs and bread could be delivered. My uncle Francis assisted the local farmer and some miners to reach the stranded families. Weeks later the drifts still curled like frozen waves along the road above my head.

Prospect House had only an outdoor closet. It was built of brick with an arched doorway, a cold place on a wintry day. A string holding squares of newspaper hung from a nail near the door. Immediately adjacent was the ash pit. It had a matching arch, a pleasing architectural feature for the times. Somewhere close by there was a chicken coop and some sheds, one of which provided shelter for a Tramp. He arrived at irregular intervals and did odd jobs, sleeping on a pile of sacking and newspapers. My mother gave him fried egg on toast and the egg used to drip down his beard. He had twinkling eyes in a weather beaten face and huge hands that he wiped across his mouth, smacking his lips with appreciation.

The local farm was Greenway Hall, and it and the nearby hillside was my play area. There was a large cobbled yard and pump with a lead lined trough. Another pump was worked in the stone-flagged kitchen. Here the water flowed into buckets that were tipped into a large shallow sink, but first a tall thin white enamelled jug was filled to top up the kettle on the hob. There were always puppies and kittens on the rag rugs, and an elderly black and brown collie lived outside. How I loved that dog! I once hid at the back of her kennel after some trouble at home, and was only discovered after a long and worrying search. Jean Brown, the farmer's daughter and I were too young at this period to attend the Hollies Private School. We played together and soon became familiar with the downhill walk to the small Baptist Chapel now used for the school. Jean became a pupil in 1935, a year after I started school. We spent a lot of time together in those early years.

Daphne Ratcliffe (nee Robinson) attended the Hollies from April 1931 to

July 1936. She remembers having lessons in the Chapel schoolroom in Fowlers Lane at Baddeley Edge. She and the other pupils were taken to see the foundations of the new school under construction at Jack Hayes Lane, Light Oaks, where she would spend the main part of her early school years. She recalls being taught by Mrs Bird who was "round faced and kind, but firm. She wore long skirts. Miss Bird had sharper features". She remembers my mother and sister Nora, John and Peter Phillips who came from Milton, Mary Lyth from Yew Tree, Jean Bradley whose father owned the Milton Bus Services, Joyce Grindey from Bagnall, Christine Holdcroft from Stockton Brook and Hazel Hodgkiss from Abbey Hulton." Some children had to change buses and then walk a considerable distance to reach school. Daphne was another pupil who went on to the Orme.

Elizabeth Wood also attended the school in its brief time at the chapel. She and her sister Catherine, affectionately known to all as Paddy, went to the Hollies from April 1932 to 1937, Paddy leaving the following year. Recalling her school days Elizabeth writes, "Paddy was four years old at the time. We travelled by Milton Bus Service to Light Oaks - quite a journey in those days. In the winter the bus invariably got stuck from Spout Lane onwards and all the children had to walk in deep snow to school. We also had quite a way to walk to the Chapel where the school was held at that time. Here my memories are of the 'pot stove' issuing forth large puffs of smoke when it was windy".

(It was a coke fired stove that towered above me at the age of four, and I can still recall the smell of fumes and the heat it emitted at close quarters).

Elizabeth continues, "At the chapel we were taught tables which we learnt 'by heart', and writing by first doing 'pot-hooks' in a special book with five lines. This was to accommodate 'upper and lower case' (letters) that we eventually joined up, the basis of 'copper plate'. One had to practice over and over again to get it right. There was no moving on to the next stage until acceptance had been achieved. Our reading lessons were often after another walk to Prospect House where Mrs. Bird had endless patience with us. Here 'leaving the room' was quite a trip to the 'loo' built to one side of the house on the ridge of the hill."

"Then the school moved to Light Oaks to a new building with the

Bird / Brown family home next door. This new school building was light and airy with a cloakroom, flush toilets and a large play area that extended to the field with Miss Bird's goats. The curriculum was very wide and encompassed Geography, History, Scripture, English Literature, Sewing and Singing - in fact, Paddy and I have said what a good grounding it was for Senior School and Further Education. Sometimes the knowledge we had acquired was not taught until we had reached the third form at Grammar school. Paddy still has a Hollies School text book called *High Roads of Tales of Literature, Book III,* which includes the history of the English Language, Latin, French and Chaucer's English which is illustrated by painters of the day. I still have a Mathematics book which I referred to when trying to instil some arithmetic into my own children".

"Exercises, hymns and prayers began the day. The first hymn I remember singing was *There is a green hill far away.* Discipline was strict inside the classroom. Talking during lessons was not tolerated and disobedience was checked in the last resort by the cane. My sister still remembers an incident! I am sure we are all grateful, looking back, as we all learnt to respect older people. Boisterous ways of letting off steam were for 'break times'. I vividly remember singing *All through the Night* at a school Prize Giving, started by one note from a tuning fork. Poetry was learnt 'off by heart'. I remember my sister reciting *The Charge of the Light Brigade* all the way through on Christmas Day in front of my Grandparents, Aunts and Uncles. They were truly amazed!"

"One could say that we were all children from similar backgrounds whose parents wished us to be educated well from the start and were willing to pay. I have a recollection of a two pounds two shilling fee being mentioned at home but I think there was a reduction because there were two of us. This sum seems very little for the good grounding we all acquired. Paddy and I were followed to The Hollies by four of our cousins, Joyce Grindey and John, Nigel and Ann Wood. Other pupils I recall were Mary and John Goodwin, Jean and Frank Bradley, John Sherratt, Pat and Michael Heard, Kenneth Moss, Daphne Robinson, Kathleen Holdcroft, Jean Bates, Christine Robson, Barbara Blagg, and Noel Lyth who sadly died. It is important to note that our social activities, visiting friends' homes and attending parties outside school hours were very valuable."

Elizabeth has several prizes of which she is very proud, handwritten on the inside cover by Miss P. M. Bird 'For Persevering Work' with the Hollies School embossed in gold lettering on the cover. The first one she received was *Stories to Read and to Tell - for little ones of nine and ten (1933-34) by Fanny Coe.*

She adds, "I shall ever be grateful to my parents and to the Bird/Brown family for launching me on my quest into acquiring knowledge and appreciating life. In my 70's one realises that to open a child's eyes to knowledge is one of the greatest gifts of a teacher". When she moved to the village of Almeley, her new home had previously been called The Hollies, a name that she reinstated. Such are the value of memories!

CHAPTER 4

I cannot recall a time when I thought of the Hollies School as anything but a part of my home, an annex to which I had access all the year round, as did every other member of the family. My name Dorothy Brown was entered in the school admittance register in January 1934 although I had shared some activities in the Baptist Chapel before the new premises at Light Oaks were ready for occupation. I believe the foundations of our house and the school were laid simultaneously but I can only recall the site on completion when there was no visible boundary between the two building lots.

There were only a few homes along Jack Hayes Lane in those days. It was a narrow turning off the slightly wider road that connected Milton and Bagnall, and led up over miles of moorland to a few isolated cottages and farms. A narrow strip of land on our side of the lane was available for development, and it was offered to my Uncle Francis for ten pounds. He turned it down as it was felt that the family had a large enough piece of land surrounding the new house and school. In retrospect it was an unfortunate decision, but in the early 1930s it required a shrewd business head to see the potential of a swampy stretch of moor land, and my family were intellectual philanthropists with little business acumen.

The boundary between our land and the moor was a ditch that was supposed to drain off the surplus ground water. My Aunt Phyllis dug out another ditch at right angles over the next two years. I tagged along as her little assistant. She gave me my earliest concept of different soils, for there was a sticky clay barely a spit below the surface. Some of the lumps she hefted out were suitable for making pottery, and she showed me how to make coil and pinch pots that we dried in the sun. Perhaps it was then I became aware of the Stoke-on-Trent Potteries for I found a piece of 'fritting' in the soil. Many years later I discovered that there had been a secret pot-making establishment in the area where the art of salt glazing had been developed. It was a daring venture set against the wealth and power of the Pottery owners of an earlier time.

Sewage from the house and school flowed into the boundary ditch until two septic tanks were constructed which my aunt surrounded with banks of turf covered with flowers. We used to sit amidst those tiny flowers to read and draw. As trees and shrubs were grown to replace the sedge and moorland vegetation, the concrete cover of the tank serving the house became a perfect spot for 'hide and seek', and was also a refuge for hedgehogs, weasels, birds and other wild life.

My Aunt spent much of her time outside school hours battling with the encroaching moor land. She was a small but very determined lady and over the years made the land very productive. Fruit bushes, rhubarb and apple trees were planted. A pear tree was trained against the back wall of the house. Our own mushrooms sprouted from the compost heap of goat and hen manure. A hedge of wild roses hid the ditch she had made and a hawthorn hedge grew between our land and the moor. For some years, cows used to break through and waded across the evil smelling mud to continue up towards the house and school. We would then rush out en masse to chase them back. The farmer added further strands of barbed wire to the original boundary posts but they sank into their swampy foundations and were lost amidst the growing shrubs. I could always find a place through which to scramble, though I had to be careful not to slip and put a foot in the sludge.

On the school side of the property a cement playground had been laid, and below the septic field concrete slabs formed the base for sheds and other buildings. Throughout my childhood, these housed goats, calves, hens, ducks, a pig and a succession of smaller animals, rabbits, tortoises, hedgehogs, and a pet owl. I kept mice, too. They frequently escaped and were caught by our cats. These animals were a bone of contention between my mother and my aunt, the former determined to uphold the family's former social position and the latter equally determined to enjoy her hobby. My Aunt encouraged my love of animals, at the same time providing milk, eggs and meat for the family. Some of my happiest memories were in and around the goat sheds. I greatly admired my aunt especially when she was shovelling out the straw and manure, or making platforms for the animals to stand upon to protect them from foot rot. She was very handy with the saw, and turned out new desks for the school or rabbit hutches with equal ability. I remember accompanying her in those (to me) carefree pre-war days as she carried a lighted storm-lamp down the garden on a dark winter's night to milk the goats. Liberal quantities of sweet smelling hay were tossed into their racks, and my aunt squatted beside each goat in turn, their lumpy shadows on the wall behind her as I watched and listened to the rhythmic musical sound of the milk squirting into the pail. The goat in the next stall would move restlessly as it waited its turn and she would murmur something to it in a gentle voice. Later the milk was strained through a piece of muslin in the school kitchen, and the jugs put on a stone slab in the small pantry to cool overnight.

The school building consisted of one long room with a coal fireplace in the middle of the inside wall. Two eight-inch water pipes ran the length of the opposite wall, the water heated by a small coke boiler. A huge kettle and a couple of pans of water always stood on the flat top ready for mixing the animals' bran mash or washing the goats' udders before the evening milking. The small furnace room was at one end of a greenhouse, built against the rear wall of the schoolroom. It overlooked the playground and lost many panes of glass over the years from misdirected balls or the occasional top. Wooden tops were very popular. We lashed them around the cement with leather thongs on sticks. When the school windows were open the air was heavy with the scent of tomato plants and chrysanthemums. Later, when rabbit meat became a welcome addition to meagre wartime rations, hutches were installed below the wooden plant stands, no doubt adding to the heady aromas.

The other half of the building consisted of a small entrance hall with the girls' toilet, a kitchen combined with a cloakroom, a pantry, coal and coke store where the cats gave birth to their kittens, and an outside toilet for the boys. There was a bathroom upstairs and an unfurnished bedroom containing a couple of armchairs and a beautiful Victorian clock on a shelf above the small fireplace. The schoolroom had a flat roof with a low parapet. Balls often landed in this cavity, an area that could be reached by climbing the down-water pipe near the front door. I do not recall anyone getting into trouble for retrieving balls, and I often went up there in my early years. My Aunt had intended to build more rooms in this space but the onset of the war prevented the completion of her plans.

My grandmother Annis, then aged seventy, was still teaching when we moved to Light Oaks. She used to stand before the large blackboard on its heavy wooden easel, a stick in her hand to draw attention to what she had written. Her glasses were usually pushed up onto her forehead, her grey hair drawn back into a bun at the nape of her neck, and a dark grey skirt discreetly covering her ankles. She had infinite patience with the younger children who sat at small desks at the front of the room. Taller desks occupied by the older ones stood at the back. At a time when children sat two at a desk in the village schools, individual desks of different sizes to accommodate each child were much appreciated.

My aunt, so loving and patient with me in the garden, was very strict in the classroom. Laziness, rudeness or a lack of attention was corrected with a swipe of the ruler on one's open palm or a rap on the knuckles, and she could be very fierce with the older boys. Punishment was invariably deserved and one tried not to offend again. Like many others I remember spending long hours practising pothooks before progressing to cursive writing. I also recall learning long paragraphs from the Bible, something I did not enjoy half so much as the long narrative poems we committed to memory. We enjoyed the daily morning hymn that we selected in turn, and my aunt put a lot of energy into her rendition. It was some years before a piano was squeezed into the schoolroom although we had always had one in the house. I believe it replaced a gramophone with a winding handle and a large record cabinet below the turntable. At one stage I could hide inside it and eavesdrop on adult conversations. Most lessons were enjoyable and introduced in a way that made one want to learn more. Sometimes as a special treat, the whole school would listen to my mother reading Greek, Indian or Scandinavian legends. I was very small when first I heard the heroic saga of Beowulf. Jeanie helped with reading and writing lessons, too, the house providing further teaching space.

In poor weather the desks were pushed back and we did physical exercises, the little ones at the front and the oldest at the back where they could be relied upon not to touch the hot pipes. "Arms up, down, up, down, feet astride, heels together, jump left, jump right, touch your toes, stand up straight". It was good fun, and on warm sunny days we did it outside. My aunt gradually created flowerbeds separated by shrubs and little winding paths behind the school and house. At first children were confined to the playground, but gradually we were allowed to make use of these precious areas. I recall one term when every playtime was used to enact an adventure story. Perhaps it was inspired by something we had been reading for we divided up into Cavaliers and Roundheads and plotted each other's downfall. The school hand-bell summoning us back to our lessons was an unwelcome interruption and we could hardly wait to get outside again to continue our adventure.

There were about twenty-four pupils at this time, ranging from four to fifteen years. We had a lean-to shelter at the back of the school parallel with the greenhouse, and we played there in wet weather. It was popular with the older girls who did not participate in our wild and noisy activities. It was a refuge, too, for timid newcomers. The shelter served as temporary storage for deliveries of bales of hay and straw. They made useful benches, as did the stone steps that led down to the playground. On rare occasions, we were allowed to take our work outside, sitting quietly on the steps in the sunshine.

Joan Millington (nee Doorbar) attended The Hollies from April 1934 to July 1936. She recalls that she was at school with me, Jean Bates, Ann and John Wood, Audrey Lovatt, Mary Goodwin who lived at the bottom of Bagnall Road, Eileen Johnson, Rose Pointon, and Barry Cooper. Joan told me that she remembered the summer uniform, a dark blue dress with a large white collar. The collars were detachable for daily washing and were easily tacked on again, a job girls had to do for themselves as soon as they were able. There would be a number of changes in the uniform as the years went by, but at this time, our winter uniform was a navy blue tunic with a girdle worn over a blouse with a tie.

Rosemary Robson attended The Hollies from January 1935 to July 1939. When I gave her the dates from the school register, she said that her mother had taught her at home for much longer than she had thought. Rosemary writes, "I can visualise your aunt and grandmother and the big schoolroom lengthways to the garden and the position of the cloakroom. The garden was steep for a time and I cannot remember any playground!" Memory is a strange thing for I recall my playmate Rosemary as an active participant in our Cavaliers and Roundheads and similar games. The playground with the steps leading down to it must have been added at least a year after the opening of the new school. Rosemary says that we wore scarlet blouses under our navy tunics. She mentions the 'endless copybooks' and comments "I can still write the alphabet perfectly if I try in the cursive style then taught and won a school prize at some time. I think it may have been for handwriting but unfortunately, the book has been lost. The journey from Endon where I lived to school at Light Oaks (and to the Orme later through the War) is in marked contrast to present day journeys. We must have changed buses in Milton because I remember buying sweets 'dolly mixtures' there after getting my three-pence pocket money."

Rosemary recalls that she was "at school with Frank Bradley of the brown buses, Barbara Anderson, Eileen Johnson, and Gordon Moore, the boy who got his pocket money, bought sweets, ate the lot and was sick"! (Rosemary, Barbara and I all went to a party at Eileen's home.)

Rosemary told me that she had a weird memory of someone who walked in their sleep, went to the garden, cut a cabbage, brought it back and put it straight into a saucepan on the stove with no water. My mother had apparently heard her and averted a catastrophe. This story of a former domestic servant must have been recounted in such a dramatic style that it appeared to have just taken place. There was no room for a live-in maid at Light Oaks. Domestic help was recruited locally for a few hours each day. My mother and Uncle Francis were great story-tellers. Francis was very theatrical, too, and could be very entertaining, though it was only on rare occasions that he was present during a Hollies' school day.

Plate 9   *The Hollies School*

Bagnall Cross, a view little changed through the early 1930s.

The Rev. Bird seated in his library, showing books, paintings and furniture that became a familiar part of the Hollies School.

Children pose for a photograph outside the Hollies School, Light Oaks, mid 1930s.

Joan Doorbar in the summer uniform of the mid 1930s, Panama hat with red ribbon and Hollies School badge and dress with huge Quaker collar.

An outing of Bagnall parishioners. Francis Bird is seen in the back row far right.

Plate 13   *The Hollies School*

Local children stand by Bagnall Cross.

Some Light Oaks residents including Jeanie Brown (second from left) and Annis Bird (centre)

More local faces, Light Oaks and Bagnall mid 1940s.

Francis Bird, youth hostelling with niece Dorothy Brown and some Smallthorne boys.

Sports at Smallthorne.

Scenes from Milton theatricals, Bagnall Choir, Youth Hostelling and the Youth Club Camp

CHAPTER 5

Light Oaks had no public house, church or telephone, the nearest being at Bagnall, but the village was by the mid 1930s gradually expanding. New houses were being built, the few original buildings bestowing an old world charm on our country lane. The house opposite ours, occupied by the Prestons, was almost hidden behind tall untrimmed hedges. An old sycamore tree to which our front gate was attached obscured it completely. The tree carried a sign for the Hollies School, too, although our house was called 'Moorside' and my Aunt's building was next door. The postman always put anything addressed to The Hollies through our letter-box.

Prestons' garden was a jungle of mature shrubs that had almost over-grown the path from their front gate. It led around the side of the house to a paved courtyard and the back porch. Occasionally I was given milk, eggs and tomatoes to take to the elderly couple and I still recall the experience. The air was heavy with the scent of flowering shrubs and the decay of fallen leaves on soil, which never caught the sun and the undergrowth was full of movement and bird song. I must have been warned about their well as I was so afraid of falling into it that I kept to the edge of the yard by an old red brick wall that separated it from the rest of the garden.

At the Bagnall Road end of the lane where the hourly bus stopped, there was a small village shop run by Mrs. Peacock. She was elderly, with iron-grey hair scraped back into a bun and long drab clothes. When one entered the shop, a hand-bell on a length of twine over the door summoned her or her husband from the backroom. She referred to him as 'the Master' and he seemed a grim intimidating figure. The counter held rows of tall glass jars with bull's eyes, acid drops, aniseed balls and chunks of homemade treacle toffee. There was also a sideways squatting open jar full of black and white humbugs. If I were the only customer she would reach over the counter and pop one into my mouth. I had a great affection for her, and could never understand why she responded to any query with "I'll see what the Master says". My family held her in high regard and when another shop opened next door to hers they were full of anxiety. The new shop had the first ice-cream making machine I had ever seen and had more capacity for provisions. Over the years it must have taken away much of her livelihood.

On the opposite side of Jack Hayes Lane there was a large house occupied by Miss Mollat who had links with the Pottery industry, and played the violin. Her house was full of interesting things like a painted ostrich egg and a large brass dinner gong. The Second World War, still some years away, proved very traumatic for her, and whenever the sirens sounded she would rush along the lane and seek shelter with my family. We got to know her very well.

There was a huge stone barn immediately next door to her property. It had the usual tall entrance for hay-wains. The cavernous interior was very dark and some of us got into trouble on one occasion for going inside. I received a sound spanking! Perhaps it was in a dangerous condition for soon it was demolished, the rough blocks being carted away for use on neighbouring farms. The land was sold and the picturesque building was replaced by several semi-detached council properties. At the same time private houses in a variety of shapes and sizes gradually filled in the gaps along the lane, ending at a cluster of old cottages.

There were very few cars. Large workhorses pulled the farm wagons, and milk was delivered by pony and trap, the farmer ladling milk into each customer's jug or can with gill, half pint or pint measures. These hung down on the inside of the churn, their curved handles hooked over the rim. A horse drawn vehicle delivered hardware, the pots and pans rattling from their hooks on the sides. Possibly the same man delivered our oil, for my mother now had a three burner oil stove with a box oven as well as a freestanding American range. Later a Raeburn and an electric stove were installed, both essential for the preparation of the midday meals she provided for the school.

From time to time Travellers' caravans passed along Jack Hayes Lane on their way up to the moor where they camped. The vans had elaborately painted doors and side panels with a horse between the shafts and ponies often tethered to the rear. The undersides of the vehicles carried a miscellany of objects, pails, kettles and baskets with livestock. The women would sometimes call at the house with pegs, lace and other handmade items to sell. When they stayed in the vicinity for several days, I could reach their camp from the bottom of the garden. There was a field to cross, then a marsh rich in marigolds and watercress, which one could safely eat in those days, and a stretch of sedge and moor land with shrubs and stunted oaks rising to a ridge. Once there I could lie on the edge of an old quarry and watch the Travellers' comings and goings. Childlike, I envied their apparent carefree existence, and never considered where they had come from, where they were going or the reason for their journey.

I have some poignant memories of those years. My father's unexpected appearance in 1935 threw the house into turmoil. It must have had some impact on the school as he arrived in the middle of lessons. He came with the resolve of taking my sister and I back to Canada but as he had made no provision for our support over the years, a role fulfiled by our uncle, his stay was brief. It was an exciting episode for a six year old, but a disturbing one for the rest of the family. On subsequent visits to England, he stayed with relatives and we visited him there. He was a romantic figure in his long fur winter coat and the Stetson he wore in milder weather. He drank whiskey and smoked cigars, a heady combination for a child growing up in a somewhat puritanical and teetotal household. During my grandmother's lifetime, card games that might lead to gambling were forbidden, and we were not allowed to play with balls or do skipping on a Sunday, only quieter activities such as reading, jigsaws, embroidery or stamp collecting.

My father's visit may have been prompted by the Silver Jubilee celebrations. I remember the bonfires and the commemorative mugs we all received. The following year King George V died, being succeeded though not for long by his son Edward VIII. My grandmother died, too, the first family bereavement I had experienced, an event that quite over-shadowed the fact that we had a new king George VI. Our home was strange without her familiar presence.

When the family house was built, it comprised three downstairs rooms, a hall, under-stairs pantry and kitchen. The front room was the library, the room next door a bedroom shared by my aunt and grandmother. The third room, behind the kitchen and overlooking the garden was the 'morning-room'. It was a cosy room, popular at all times of the day, with a boiler behind the fireplace to heat the water. My sister Nora, foster sister Jean and I shared the large front bedroom. The back room was my uncle's den. My mother used the 'box-room', an inadequate space as it housed the chest containing my grandfather's sermons. She kept her typewriter there, too, as she was writing a novel. It was finished but she never sent that particular book to a publisher.

The first of a series of structural changes was the addition of a lean-to kitchen and enclosed porch. This extended to the boundary of my aunt's property and was the cause of some disagreement. As always Francis's humour and common sense saved the day when his sisters disagreed. The new back door was only a few steps from the school furnace room, an area sheltered by a shed housing the coal and firewood for the house. My aunt was quick to acknowledge that it would provide a short cut for everyone in bad weather. The old kitchen now became a small schoolroom, used for reading lessons and private study. Examinations were held there, the papers put into a sealed envelope and hand-delivered to the headmaster of Bagnall School. They were then forwarded with his own to the appropriate authority.

When my grandmother died, my aunt moved to the upstairs room in the Hollies. This had been furnished as a bedroom for my father during his brief visit. My aunt used the room from then on until her health began to deteriorate and my mother insisted that she returned to the house, the morning room becoming her bedroom. The wall between the two main rooms had been removed, replaced by a folding partition. By then the library had become the school dining room, and the backroom turned into an additional schoolroom. Both rooms still had the old family furnishings, my grandfather's oil paintings and Victorian ornaments. The partition was folded back to make one large room when required.

The large front bedroom was also partitioned to form another small room. Boarders had been inevitable. There was always some child in need of a temporary home due to illness or bereavement in the family. Missionaries' children occasionally stayed for a few weeks, and one eleven year old boy would eventually stay for a much longer period. Gerloff was Dutch, a child traumatised by his experiences in World War II whom the family nursed back to health. There were many occasions when my mother gave up her bedroom. She kept a supply of bedding in a downstairs cupboard and no one seemed to question where she slept. It seems to have been on the floor!

The library was a convenient place for many local meetings. The Bucknall parish still had a strong link with the family from my grandfather's days. Children from the rectory invariably attended the Hollies School, and although the parsonage of St. Chad's church, Bagnall was only a few minutes' walk away in Light Oaks Avenue, our house provided a meeting room for the Church of England's Men's Society and the Sunday Bible Class. Parish outings, youth hostelling trips and the possible need for air raid precautions were all discussed behind the closed partition. I never questioned this frequent use of our living space but I do recall on at least one occasion feeling disappointed that I could not get a reference book I needed.

Jeanne Townend (nee Bates) attended The Hollies from September 1937 to September 1941, a time when so many aspects of our lives would change and never be the same again. Gas masks had been issued, the first evacuees left London, and bacon, butter and sugar were rationed. From a child's perspective, we would soon be enjoying Disney's 'Snow White and the seven dwarfs', and 'Sabu, the elephant boy', at one of the cinemas in Hanley, films I remember with delight. 'Whistle while you work' became very popular.

Jeanne writes, "I went to the Hollies when I was $4^1/_2$ and left when I was $8^1/_2$ to go to the Orme Girls' School. My memories of the school (we called it Birdies) are very happy. We used to go into Mrs. Brown's house for reading. I still have two books I received as prizes that have The Hollies School imprinted into the hard covers.

I lived in Abbey Hulton and travelled up to Light Oaks twice daily on the Bagnall bus. We used to love it in the winter when the snow was too thick for the bus to reach Light Oaks and we had to slither and slide down the hill to Milton.

I remember the large schoolroom with Miss Bird's desk at one side next to the stove and the blackboard easel in the middle". (For a time a Valor stove was used to heat the room. Perhaps there was a shortage of coal!) Jeanne recalls sitting behind a girl with very long plaits and dipping the ends in her inkwell! Screws of paper were also sometimes dipped in an inkwell and flicked across the room with a ruler. The punishment for such a crime must have been severe, but perhaps Jeanne's mischief went undetected. The floorboards and desks were covered with ink-stains, but pen nibs spluttered and pens frequently rolled off the sloping desks. Mothers must have lost patience on many occasions because of ink on school uniforms.

Jeanne goes on to say, "Miss Bird must have taught us well as I could parse a sentence though I am not sure that I can today! We did long division and fractions and complicated money sums in the old money (£.s.d.). I remember going out on to the concrete yard where we lined up facing each other to play 'Here we go gathering nuts in May' and 'A farmer's in his Den'.

Sometimes we would go with Miss Bird to take her goats to a nearby field. If we were good, we were allowed to hold a tether and lead one. Once a goat got loose and we all ran after it down the road.

Every week we had a handicraft lesson. One week we chose what we wanted to do and the next week we had to knit vests for Jewish refugees. I did not like knitting. I dropped stitches on purpose and had to go to Miss Bird to pick them up. Then I was able to stand by the warm stove and the lesson went quickly! My vest became pale grey and took weeks to finish!" (Bagnall Parish had close links with the China Inland Mission, Palestine and the Church Mission for the Jews, and my Aunt supported missionary work all her life.)

Jeanne recalls, "A sad memory I have is of the people next door to the school. One morning we were told that the small toddler there had fallen into a tub of water and drowned. It was very disturbing". (It was indeed.) The mother had been called to the door while she was washing clothes in the dolly tub. When my aunt broke the news to the school there was a stricken silence. Counselling did not exist in our childhood and it was not long before our school day continued as usual. Whatever happened, life just went on.

Jeanne's comment about 'the Birdies' reminded me of an incident one dark evening in Jack Hayes Lane. Some of the neighbouring children who attended Bagnall School gathered outside our gate and mischievously began to sing:

Let's all sing like the Birdies sing, give yourself a treat,
Let's all sing like the Birdies sing, tweet, tweet, tweet tweet tweet!

As they continued their prank, my mother and aunt began to get angry. Uncle Francis put his cap on and went outside. A few minutes later, he was singing the same refrain, just as heartily. The children held him in great respect and never bothered the family again.

CHAPTER 6

Valerie Whittaker (nee Sylvester) attended The Hollies from April 1940 until July 1944. She writes, "I was eight years old when I started and I had previously attended the village school at Bagnall. There were only about thirty pupils aged 4 to 14. Miss Bird taught us all but we went to the house next door to Mrs Brown for reading. I think that there were about four other children at my level. Some of the boys and girls had to travel several miles to school.

I was very proud of my uniform. I wore a red berry with a badge showing a piece of holly on it. A red long sleeved knitted jumper over a white blouse and red tie was worn in the winter with a navy tunic and red girdle. In the Summer, I wore a navy dress with a white Quaker collar and a red ribbon bow at the neck. We had to change into indoor shoes when we arrived at school.

We were all taught in the same classroom at desks of different heights according to our size. All age groups did singing, art and games together. I did not like singing. We were taught tonic sol-fa and had to sing up and down the scale. Then Miss Bird would ask a pupil to sing whichever note she pointed to. I did like art and we often drew using pastels. We were taught to observe shadows and to crayon them in. I still have my sketchbook. We were allowed to go and sit on the stairs to learn poetry. One poem that I remember was:

> 'Up the airy mountain,
> down the rushy glen,
> we daren't go a hunting
> for fear of little men'

We used to put on a concert at Christmas time. I remember being 'Old Mother Hutch who walked with a crutch' in one play, and Adolf Hitler's wife in another. It was during the Second World War. Mrs. Brown wrote the plays that we performed. My school days were happy ones. I wonder now how Miss Bird taught the children of such varying ages. Discipline was not a problem. I did find a difference when I started at a Grammar School with 600 girls when I was eleven years' old". Valerie went on to the Orme Girls' School.

Maureen Leese (nee Kelsall) attended The Hollies from the early spring of 1941 to the end of November 1942. She writes "My family moved from Basford to a bungalow at Yew Tree ('Fairfields') in 1941 to escape the bombs falling on Shelton Bar, only to have one fall even closer at Carmountside! We only lived at Yew Tree for a short time so I recall little about school apart from having to drink goats' milk at break. I remember Mr. and Mrs. Marsh who lived opposite us, Pat Bevington, the Mayer family from the farm, Val Sylvester and the Walker's who kept St. Bernard dogs".

Jacqueline Walker lived at 'Woodlands', Bagnall Road, and her name was entered in the school register in 1941. I visited the house on a number of occasions with my aunt. The huge dogs were a great attraction! The farm was just above them on the Bank, the local name for Bagnall Road. I recall an occasion when I was sent down to the farm for milk. Perhaps we had a visitor who disliked goats' milk! I had been given a small metal can with a lid. The farmer filled it to the brim, and it dripped all the way home as the can swung from the thin handle. I must have been very conscious of the waste to remember such a trivial detail.

Maureen's father Eric Kelsall was a Special Constable during their stay at Yew Tree. I imagine that he shared some of the work of Mr. Hughes, the Constable for Light Oaks and Bagnall. Eric had to patrol the lonely moorland roads, a job he found somewhat unnerving.

He will have called in at the Wardens' Post at the Hollies, for from 1939 onwards part of the building had been used for this purpose. The outside wall of the school kitchen was reinforced with sandbags. An emergency stretcher was secured to the cloakroom wall with the children continuing to hang their outdoor clothes on the pegs protruding through its bright green mesh. Protective clothing in case of a Mustard Gas attack was housed in one corner and there was a stirrup pump and a bucket of sand for fire fighting. A box held information leaflets on such matters as The Duties of Air Raid Wardens, First Aid, and Personal Protection Against Gas. My uncle had a metal helmet and a special gas mask with goggle eyes and a corrugated nozzle from the nosepiece, and he kept a gas proof Baby Container with a hand-pump in his bedroom. The wardens soon abandoned the school cloakroom for the comfort of our front room and my mother provided such refreshments as were possible due to rationing.

Christine Botham (nee Lord) attended The Hollies from April 1941 to July l944.

She says, "We lived in Bagnall and it was my first school. It was run by Miss Bird and Mrs. Brown, and I recall it as a fun school. We had to lie on blankets on the floor after lunch to recover from our activities, one of which I remember particularly. Miss Bird kept goats and if we went to school early, we could help in taking them down the road to the field where they were tethered for the day. We learnt to socialise by going to each other's Birthday Parties, and I know I have a 'twin' with whom I shared the same birthday. I remember being in a school play, and the only words I spoke were 'This is Lord Haw Haw speaking'!"

This is obviously the same play featuring Adolph Hitler's wife played by Valerie Sylvester, and must have had tremendous parental appeal. My uncle and mother possibly joined forces in creating this comedy. He kept a tub of children's theatrical costumes, mostly home-made, in his room, and before any Smallthorne or Hollies' theatrical production they were brought downstairs, sorted through, laundered and repaired by my mother.

My uncle Francis enjoyed amateur theatre and was a member of the Milton drama group. I recall one evening when the wire holding the curtains snapped in the middle of a performance in which I had a small part. The plays were always light-hearted affairs and on that occasion, the evening was an instant success. The Hollies' school plays, originally performed in the big schoolroom but later in the house, were much appreciated, too.

Peter Sherratt attended The Hollies from April l94l to April 1943. He recalls sadly that his brother John, who was a pupil between 1936 and 1940 died in 1984 at the age of 53. John was one of my contemporaries. .

Peter writes, "I remember well Miss Bird, Francis Bird and Mrs. Brown. My father, John Charles Sherratt, was a Headmaster, and a Lay Reader at St. Chad's, Bagnall. He died in l974 aged 70. I was the Organist at St.

Chad's for eleven years, but since 1981 have been Organist at St. Philip & St. James' Church in Milton. A life long member of the Church of England I married a priest's daughter forty years ago. Apart from the great influence of my father, my adherence to Christianity is due in some means to Phyllis Marion Bird. I received a deep Christian grounding at The Hollies with particular schooling in the Old Testament, unusual by today's standards.

There was a sort of 'kindly' anti-Jewish ethos! We were encouraged to bring pennies and halfpennies to school to place in a box labelled 'Mission to the Jews', presumably to encourage them to convert to Christianity. I also remember a cane, of the garden variety, standing in the corner of the big schoolroom, but I never remember it being used. We boys were treated firmly, but kindly. For Nature Study, on one occasion we observed the goats in the garden, and then took them along Jack Hayes Lane to drink at a well The registers were called before we went home in the afternoon, and each would shout, 'Present all day, Miss Bird', if such was the case".

The well Peter mentions was known to us as The Wishing Well, and unfortunately has now disappeared. We used to drink from the clear flowing water when we passed it if the local 'witch' was not in the vicinity. This poor woman lived in a wooden cabin set back among the trees, and was always dressed in black. She wore narrow boots with countless buttons and seemed very old as she hobbled to the well to collect her water. It never crossed our minds to help her carry her pails, though she would no doubt have refused assistance. I was afraid of her!

Peter continues, "My little friend was Ian Gardener, son of the Rector of Bucknall, and Christine Lord from Bagnall Hall Farm. Ian was at The Hollies from October 1939 to January 1942. He became a Priest, and died in 2001. My Brother John's friend was Nigel Wood (September 1936 to July 1940). He became a vet. Jean Bates was his friend, too. Another school friend was Michael Heard (January 1941 to July 1946). His father was the doctor in Milton. One day Miss Bird said, 'Michael, you of ALL PEOPLE have spelt 'surgery' - 'sugary'. I remember the incident well!

On another occasion, we put on a play based on an Old Testament story. A small sapling was placed in a stone pot, under which I sheltered. Francis Bird, dressed as Moses, was most impressive! It all seemed so realistic to me. I remember my father, Dr. Heard and Rector Gardener clapping loudly at the end. I also recall being presented with a book at prize giving, entitled *The Sandhill Stag*. When I got it home it was inscribed 'Dorothy Cartlidge for Perseverance' I had been given the wrong prize, but I kept it just the same!!!" (Dorothy and her brother Brian were at The Hollies from 1941 to 1943 and 1945.)

"We lived at Yew Tree, half way between Milton and Bagnall. I went up the hill on the bus, a halfpenny ticket, and walked home. One winter the snow was so deep that I had to be carried home by the Curate from Bagnall. I do not know how he became involved. I remember being frightened of the boys' lavatory and also of the buckets of water and sand that were part of the wartime precautions. I do not remember what scared me, as I was a very little boy! "

When war was declared my uncle painted the top section of all the windows in both buildings a dark blue He also criss-crossed every pane with brown tape as a precaution in case the glass shattered. The boys' toilet window, having no curtain, was painted in its entirety, making the little room very dark for many years until the paint finally flaked off.

Peter recalls that one day Miss Bird gave the assembled pupils a stern warning against congregating in groups to look into the grids of drains and drop pebbles therein. She would not punish us for disobedience, but we could expect death from diphtheria or other foul plague. There was no main drainage at this time, all the houses having septic tanks, so possibly some illness in the village had reminded her of the untimely death of her own little brother many years previously.

Peter also mentions Jack Holdcroft who had been Choirmaster at St. Chads for many years. He was one of my uncle's frequent visitors. Peter says that Jack passed away in 1975. My uncle and I had both been in the choir. I think Jack must have been a very tolerant man as I took my favourite pet mouse to church on more than one occasion, letting it run along the choir stall to another chorister who turned it round and sent it back. It possibly helped pass the time when we all had an uninteresting sermon to sit through! On Sunday evenings, once we had put on our caps and cassocks we youngsters would creep out into the graveyard and pretend to be ghosts amidst the tombstones. There was one distinctive obelisk shaped plinth that someone endowed with strange powers. If one walked around it seven times saying the Lord's Prayer backwards, the devil would appear. The idea was too wicked to even contemplate so we never put it to the test, but we did enjoy the wind at the back of the church as it blew our cassocks out around us.

Alma Mifflin (nee Gordon) attended The Hollies from April 1942 to July 1944. She told me that she was at school with Mary and Paul Bond (1939 to 1945), Allen Bottomley (l942 to 1948) and Peter Sherratt. She says that she was a small child, and was called 'Mousey' or 'Little Mouse' at school. She was a blackbird in a school play, and wore black material draped over her shoulders and arms. She remembered walking with the goats to the field and also my white mice that "lived in an old round wash-tub in the greenhouse and were covered by a dustbin lid". In describing her uniform, she refers to the white Puritan collar of the summer dress, a red blazer with the school badge on its pocket, and a Panama hat with a red band and badge. Her winter uniform included a red silk tie.

Alma remembers learning to do cursive writing in exercise books that had been cut in half. There were rows of a, b, and c which she learnt to join up, a daily task. She was very proud of her grown-up writing and was disappointed when her family had to move and she went to a new school. The teacher told her 'No child writes like this. We all print here'!

Occasionally her father brought her to school very early to fit in with his farm work. Otherwise, her mother brought her to school by bicycle. She had a little red one that must have been left at school all day. She says that they had to go down one hill and then up another one, and she thought that if she pedalled down hill fast it would help her on the upwards climb. One day she lost control and was thrown off and got a black eye. The daily journey they made was through lonely moorland, and was a long journey for a small girl. They were living at Kerryhill Farm, Bucknall, at that time. Alma mentioned that her cousin Tony Ball went to The Hollies in 1945.

CHAPTER 7

The Hollies School goats impressed many children. They were an important part of my childhood, too. On average, there were about seven as there were always new or half grown kids around. They were all from pedigree stock and my aunt's name featured in the goat breeders' manual. When she bought a new animal, it was delivered by rail to Milton station. Small farm animals travelled in the luggage van together with bicycles, bulky purchases, newspapers and mail. A goat would be tied in a corner with a bit of sacking and some straw at a safe distance from anything it might fancy as a meal. Upon reaching its destination, it was led off down a ramp by the new owner. My aunt would check its condition before taking it off along Market Street, past the doctor's house, Barclays Bank on the corner, up Bagnall Road past Yew Tree and finally home. Much to my mother's disapproval, I would often accompany her.

No former pupil has recalled the sudden demise of the large and smelly billy goat that inhabited a shed at the end of the garden. One day it severely injured my aunt's hand, temporarily disabling her. It was shot, and as meat was in such short supply, the animal was butchered and preserved in a barrel of salt. I believe that this was Uncle's idea, a seemingly good one after all the stories of life at sea that the family had shared. The joints were very well preserved for no amount of soaking or boiling could remove the saltiness, and at least some of them still encrusted with salt and almost resembling logs ended up at the back of the fireplace, supplementing the coal ration!

The next station along the line from Milton was Stockton Brook. We regarded it in the 1940s as an easy walking distance from Light Oaks, following Fowlers Lane to Baddeley Edge and then down on the other side to reach the valley. It was a very familiar route. My uncle often decided to take the family out for the day at short notice. My mother and aunt would hastily pack a picnic and we rushed off for the station, accompanied by any child who happened to be around. Many boys from Uncle's class at Smallthorne who arrived unexpectedly shared 'Sir's generosity. Our party filled a train compartment, packed into the two long seats that faced each other. Picnic bags went into the string mesh racks overhead, and one was lucky to get a corner seat by the window. Then the lucky ones got the job of closing the windows when we entered a tunnel, to open them again when the train emerged into daylight. My uncle reminded us that no one should put a head out of a window, the guard blew his whistle and off we went. He often took us to Rudyard Lake where he knew the boatman in charge of boats for hire. He had lost a hand, possibly in the First World War, and wore a large metal hook with which he was adept at steadying boats as we clambered aboard. When we returned from our long journey up the lake and back he was equally dextrous in guiding us in again with his long pole. Uncle taught countless children to row at Rudyard or Trentham Park and no doubt gave many the lasting pleasure of 'messing around in boats'.

Family excursions often commenced via Baddeley Edge and the canal at Stockton Brook. Towpaths were useful routes, and Francis seemed to know many bargees on the long boats carrying coal that we passed. They were very poor but to children there was a romance in the lives they led, living in a cabin in the stern with its small chimney stack, while the sturdy thickset horse plodded its way ahead pulling the barge along. Francis knew some of the boys in charge of the horses, and I am sure Jeanie felt relief that their work prevented them from joining the family from the school, something which could happen miles from home. The prow of the long boats and the sides of the cabins were sometimes elaborately painted with scenes of castles or flower designs, the bright colours a vivid contrast to the drab working clothes of those aboard.

An excursion by longboat was organised sometime in the 'forties for Light Oaks and Bagnall parishioners. It may have been a Choir Outing. It was a happy occasion with lots of singing, conversation and laughter. The sun shone, and mallards, coots and moorhens paddled swiftly out of our way as we glided along, with the occasional blue green flash of a kingfisher somewhere ahead, a common sight in those days.

Life at the house 'Moorside' and The Hollies was an ongoing educational experience. Throughout their lives, Francis Bird, Phyllis and Jeannie not only continued to add to their own knowledge but also never missed an opportunity of passing on relevant and interesting information.

Francis and Jeannie shared a love of history. Francis and Phyllis jointly enjoyed science, particularly zoology, biology and botany. All three enjoyed travel, often through the pages of books, which were read aloud, each taking a turn as the family sat around the fireplace through the winter months. Francis was always the most dramatic, especially when some seafaring book had been chosen, and no one objected to an interruption to explain or illustrate some passage. Adventure stories from *The Boys' Own Paper*, printed in the 1890s and rich in fact and daring deeds were very popular. They had been collected, stitched and bound by the Rev. Arthur Bird and were read and enjoyed by successive generations of children until they finally fell apart.

Learning continued outside the home and school. Francis took considerable pleasure in organising outings. Both he and Phyllis passed on the names of birds and vegetation, Phyllis particularly knowledgeable about aquatic life. Jeanie shared her appreciation of the scenery and was quick to create imaginary characters for an empty boathouse or distant farm building. Francis would follow her lead, the two of them weaving an adventure story to amuse the younger members of the party.

Every opportunity was taken to visit archeological digs, museums, historic buildings or churches. There was always an adult nearby prepared to further enrich the children's experience. During Jeanie's lifetime, she acquired a phenomenal knowledge of English history. Originally interested in anything Roman, she went on to study the lives of many historical figures, particularly writers, her anecdotes bringing them back to life with a humour seldom evident in her normal daily life. She was the serious member of our adult world. Francis had a great sense of humour, and Phyllis fluctuated between the two, as indeed she did with politics for Jeanie was very Conservative while Francis considered himself a Socialist. This could have been an insupportable situation in some establishments but the serious discussions which took place, never turned to rows, no doubt a reflection of their own childhood and the influence of Annis and Arthur Bird.

Despite the troubled times of the Second World War, and years of poor health that interrupted my attendance at Grammar School, I had an interesting childhood. The frequent periods of convalescence, largely unsupervised as my mother, uncle and aunt were teaching, gave me the opportunity to explore the local countryside. I went often to Baddeley

Edge and Bagnall, although I walked much further afield. I found the environment and the flora and fauna it contained fascinating. It was a time of personal enrichment. Alone with my dog Raf, named after the RAF for which I had much admiration, and my aunt's border collie Lady, I would set off after my mother and aunt had gone into school. Mrs.Wilshaw, the Hollies' cook at that time, prepared a picnic lunch for me as she knew that probably I would not return until the end of the school day.

I enjoyed visiting Arthur Brown's farm at Greenway Hall, and felt a proprietary right to the ancient cannon that lay on the hillside opposite Prospect House, my first English home. Sitting astride the rusty barrel propped up by a few large stones; I could look out over the valley and dream about the future. There was a short cut to Bagnall through the farmyard and across the golf course. My favourite route was the narrow pathway up through Hough Woods where a stream skirted its northern edge. It could be a creepy sort of place, supposedly haunted by some unfortunate who had been murdered and buried amidst the trees. I would not have ventured there without the dogs. One could follow the stream to its source, and then cut across to join a footpath to Bagnall. Another stream bordered the Links, and by following its meandering course, one could come out not far from the Hospital.

Bagnall Springs was another favourite place. There were sticklebacks in the stream and leeches in the shaded pool beneath the bluff. A bridge had once spanned the water linking Bagnall and Tomkin by a bridle track. Uncle told me a tale of a Jacobean fugitive who had been caught and flayed, hence the name Tom'(s)kin! Perhaps the same wretched man had expired at Endon (end of him!) in the valley. How many of these stories were local tales based on true events and how much the result of Uncle's fertile imagination I do not know. The area has many historical links with the Jacobean rebellions, and Greenway Hall, the one time home of Judge John Bradshaw, one of the gentlemen responsible for sentencing Charles I to death, was said to have sheltered refugees in 1745.

At Endon, a rebel pleaded for a drink of water from the well and as he lay dying, he prayed that it would never run dry. Like many such wells it has continued flowing and is dressed with flowers and blessed annually. One tale led to another, and as a child, I was an avid listener.

The rebel's skin was sent to Endon to be tanned in order to use it for a drum, but the skin developed a life of its own, refusing to stay immersed in the tanning pit. In the end it had to be returned to where the other remains were buried, presumably finding peace at last.

Endon's well dressing was a much-anticipated event. The well was always a work of art, but the fair was the main attraction with its noisy steam traction engine and the smell of hot grease. The local children danced around the Maypole, plaiting and unravelling the coloured ribbons. Sylvia Myatt who attended The Hollies in 1944 told me of Maypole dancing and May Queens when the blessing of a well in Spout Lane took place. She and her school friend Shirley Coe later took part in a troupe dancing team at Baddeley Edge, but I think these were post-war activities.

I do recall the Salvation Army visiting Jack Hayes Lane. They used to stand outside the house and school to play their instruments, a noisy intrusion on our quiet lane before they came to the door with the collection box. A dimmer memory is of a disabled fair-haired boy who came with a pedal organ on a horse-drawn vehicle. The organ was carried into the Hollies' schoolroom where he played hymns for some of the local ladies. This organ was not the one I later played in Bagnall church. The key to St. Chads was kept under the doormat, but sometime in the 1940s, it was put on the ledge over the door. I had to climb on the stone seat in the porch to reach it. I would let myself in with the dogs and they would lie beside me while I enjoyed the small organ, playing anything that came to mind. I used to imagine my unknown grandfather preaching from the pulpit as he had done so many times, smiling down at me.

I remember when the main organ had been pumped by hand, a chorister creeping through a panel for this duty. How it sighed and wheezed at times! With the installation of electricity, the lovely brass lamps in the Nave were taken down. When my family first moved to Jack Hayes Lane the house also had no electricity. For some time we continued to use our old brass table lamps. The school building had electric lighting so perhaps the local power supply was inadequate. The pylon in the field next to the Peacock's shop was very vulnerable to high winds and thunderstorms. When electricity was brought to the house, the wires to the switches were not set in the plaster and were covered with beading much to my mother's annoyance. She said they harboured spiders that she had disliked since her first encounter with an enormous one in the Australian bush.

The last visit my father was able to make to England came at the time of German air attacks and the fear of invasion. Serious discussions took place among the adults for plans were being made to evacuate entire schools overseas. Forms were handed out at the Orme Girls School for us to take home. Then I suddenly became aware that we would be going to Canada. My uncle, aunt and mother had apparently volunteered as escorts for school parties. I do not recall asking for details. The war years were strange and so much was happening all the time! The prospect of being nearer my father was exciting but the thought of leaving Light Oaks and my pets was most disturbing. I realise now that my uncle, aunt and mother would have returned to England while we would have been evacuated to some part of Canada possibly thousands of miles from my father's home on Vancouver Island. Their trans-Atlantic journeys would have occurred during the school holidays, and life at The Hollies would have continued as usual. It must have been a difficult decision for them all, particularly my mother. In the event, following the sinking of the 'Athenia' carrying hundreds of evacuees to the United States and the increased activity of German U-boats, the plan was abandoned. I never saw my father again. He died in Canada in 1945.

During the 1930s, my uncle had experimented with a hand-made receiving set. I first recall listening to a wireless in 1936 when Edward VIII made his abdication speech. That wireless was a large brown object, possibly two feet long and fifteen inches high. It had a large wet battery in a compartment at one end. The day following our first air raid, some miles away, it burst into flames. My mother with great presence of mind threw a rug over the burning set and dropped it through the library window. The bombing was blamed for the incident, a whimsical idea! Our new wireless was much smaller and plugged into an electric socket. The family took the daily news broadcast very seriously and no child present would have dared to speak while the wireless was switched on. I remember the tense atmosphere.

I had been staying with cousins when gasmasks were first issued. We lined up in the garden according to size to facilitate the measuring. The mask was kept in a cardboard box with a string for carrying. Then a weatherproof canvas cover was devised, an important accessory as we had to take the gasmask to school each day. Later a further bright green nosepiece was added. At the Orme we had to practice wearing the gas mask during lessons. It must have been very frustrating for teachers. I could not see through the eyepiece, as masks were not designed to accommodate glasses. I do not think anyone could view the blackboard clearly. We soon learnt how to disrupt a boring lesson by blowing into the mask, the escaping air making rude sounds that made everyone giggle. My acute myopia had only been recognised when my grandmother had tried to teach me to play the piano. I could not see the music. Until then I had been considered clumsy! There were no routine eye tests for children in those days.

The early war years saw the disappearance of many of our family treasures in response to the appeal for donations to the Spitfire fund, the little fighter monoplane designed by Reginald Mitchell of Stoke-on-Trent. It was probably at the same time that iron railings began to disappear from public places. We had to be careful not to trip over the jagged ends left protruding from the ground, particularly as weeds soon hid them from view. Air-raid shelters began to appear near bus stops in the valley. The first I recall was at Milton, just past Barclays Bank, on the road to Abbey Hulton. It was a rectangular brick and concrete box to protect travellers from shattered glass and shrapnel. Signs indicated entrances to the basements of public buildings in the towns where one could take shelter. One morning the siren started wailing when we were on our way to school. We left the bus and were taken down into the cellar of a vegetable warehouse where we sat on wooden crates until the 'All clear' sounded. It was a momentous occasion as we were all given an orange, the last imported fruit we would see for years.

Many people had Anderson shelters constructed in their gardens. An aunt of mine who lived at Basford sacrificed an entire downstairs room to a Morrison shelter. It was like a steel mesh cage, but with both sons on active service, it made her feel more secure. It took some months for the Orme Girls' School shelters to be completed. They were dug out in a zigzag pattern across our playing fields. A steep ramp led down to each interconnected section that could house thirty or more girls. We had to sit facing each other below ground, cold slabs of concrete at our backs and overhead. There was an emergency exit in the roof at each corner, but I never saw one opened. I imagine they were covered with turf.

When there was an air-raid warning, the school bell rang continuously. We had to drop whatever we were doing, line up and jog to our allotted shelter. No one minded when this occurred in the middle of a French or Latin lesson, but the worst time was during gym, an activity we practised in our blue woollen pants and white blouses. There was no time to don our thick serge tunics, and whatever the weather we sped off to the shelters to shiver until the 'All clear' sounded. Each shelter was equipped with emergency rations and these had to be replaced from time to time. There were sticks of barley sugar and Horlicks tablets, a real treat for our sugar-starved bodies.

Rations were quite inadequate in 1940 and '41, six ounces of meat per week per person, four ounces of bacon, four of butter, two of tea and twelve of sugar. My mother hoarded the family sugar in order to make jam, as did many of our neighbours. Nothing was wasted. Tea leaves were brewed again and again, and then used to pad out cake recipes. At one time, the cheese ration fell to one ounce, and even soap was limited to three ounces. As a family, we were very fortunate, due to my aunt's animals, fruit and vegetables. She obtained permission to cultivate the field that housed the electricity pylon, a no go area for the children of Light Oaks, and grew rows of potatoes, swedes and cabbages to feed the family and the school. The goats were tethered there to clear the grass before she set to work with her spade. Goat, rabbit and poultry meat, eggs and milk supplemented our meals. We experimented with butter and cheese making, but the hand turned churn was very time consuming and exhausting. My mother preserved eggs in 'water-glass', and the entire family gathered fruit from the garden and countryside. This was turned into jam or preserved in large screw-topped jars. My aunt enjoyed making chutneys and pickles, storing the jars in the school pantry for special occasions.

Much to my disappointment, I had slept through the region's first air raid. The large Aluminium Works in the valley was the target for a number of unsuccessful raids, its products important for propellers and wing coverings for military aircraft. Light Oaks was on one of the flight routes for Liverpool and Manchester and on some nights we could hear the heavy throb of the German bombers as they passed overhead. I had recurring nightmares of our staircase being blocked by an unexploded bomb. I can see it now with its nose buried in the floor by the front door and its tail fins almost level with my eyes. Uncle took me to see a friend's damaged home. The front wall had been completely blown out, leaving the rooms, bathroom, hall and furniture looking like an enormous doll's house. There was a huge crater in the road and piles of rubble, an all too familiar sight from news broadcasts these days but a shock to us in the early 1940s. Two incendiary bombs hit the Orme School, one landing on a corner of a netball court and the other burning a section of the floor at the back of the gym. The area was roped off for safety, but morning assemblies went on as usual, the rows of girls standing closer together than was customary. Little publicity was given to such incidents. Schoolchildren were quite excited when an anti-aircraft battery was installed at the top of Limekiln bank on the way to Hanley. Searchlights continuously swept the night sky, and occasionally a plane would be caught in the cross beams of light, followed by the staccato sound of guns.

On the terrible night in November, 1940, all the family stood outside on the school playground and watched the sky changing colour in the distance as wave after wave of enemy planes dropped incendiaries and explosives on far away towns. The horizon was dotted with pinpoints of light that fanned out before being absorbed in the surrounding glow. The six hundred year old Coventry Cathedral was gutted by fire, and a cousin of mine, a Stoke-on-Trent fireman who had been called there to help was one of the many who died that night.

Shortly after the outbreak of war, I had been given the use of a pony. I think the owner was on active service. It was stabled at the Grindey's of Bankhouse, Bagnall. Joyce Grindey had attended the Hollies from 1933 to 1936 before going on to the Orme Girls' School. The pony had grown fat and lazy through lack of exercise, and objected to being ridden. She unseated me time and again while I pretended she was a bucking bronco, part of my imaginary 'Canadian' life. In the end, we had many good rides although the numerous falls I had earlier suffered resulted in surgery and put a temporary end to my riding.

Meanwhile Arthur Brown and family had moved from Greenway Hall to Woodhead Farm. Jean, my old time companion, was still attending the Hollies. There was an acute shortage of labour on all the farms, and together we learnt to master her father's tractor. They were simple machines then, with forward and reverse gear and a metal steering wheel. Arthur managed his two large horses while we followed behind the team, the tractor dragging a harrow. The Evening Sentinel carried a photograph of Jean driving the tractor but my mother would not allow me to be included She was unaware of how much time I spent at Woodhead farm. It was easy to reach from the bottom of the garden and up over the moor. We played in the hayloft over the cowsheds, and on one occasion dared each other to get astride the back of a bull calf in a stall below. I tumbled into the mud, dirt that had to be explained away later in the day. On a different occasion, we discovered a cow in trouble out on the hillside. We had to find Arthur and then race to the kitchen for hot water, soap and rags. Later we watched the assisted birth, an exciting incident, as I had never been allowed in our goat sheds when the kids were delivered. Jean and I regularly fed mangel-wurzels, mangolds as they were called locally, into a huge machine that chopped them into pieces for the farm stock. It was rather like a gigantic kitchen mincer. We had to stand on a box in the barn to drop the roots on to the cutting blades. It was a dangerous activity for children, but we did a lot of dangerous things by today's standards. My aunt used to sit on the shelter steps to cut up mangolds for the goats, sharpening her knife on a hand-turned whetstone. I was allowed to pour water on the whetstone and turn the handle but was never allowed to use the knife!

Rules and regulations governed the slaughtering of farm animals, but there must have been many unreported 'deaths' across the country. In one instance Jean and I were told to deliver a letter to a distant farm. No one must see us so we had to keep to the fields as far as possible and avoid the lanes. Jean knew some animal had been killed and I felt guilty, not understanding what the secrecy was about. I knew that on this occasion I would not be able to confide in my aunt who was always interested in my farm experiences. She encouraged my love of animals, providing hutches or pens for a large variety of pets, including hedgehogs and a tawny owl that had been shot by a neighbour's lodger. It was one of the rare occasions that I heard my uncle address someone in anger. He tended the injured bird, putting its wing in a splint. It healed but the bird could no longer fly. Tawny became my pet and lived in an especially constructed cage beneath the roof of a goat shed, dying ultimately of old age. My aunt cared for all the pets during my many illnesses throughout my adolescence. My mother tolerated the various animals, but made no secret of her dislike of the goats, often expressing concern that they kept my aunt outside when it was cold or wet. She had a real fondness for our dogs and the various cats, all of them descended from one she had had at Hartshill, but when our ducks followed her in the garden or chickens scratched around her feet when she was hanging out the washing, she was not amused!

The 1940s have left many vivid memories, the sad ones softened by time but others somewhat humorous when recalled to mind. One day a stranger walked unsteadily down the path between the house and school. His clothes were creased and soiled, and he needed a shave. My mother noticed that his hands were dirty with broken nails, so was surprised by his well-educated accent when he asked if she could spare him some food. He seemed very weak so she got a chair for him to sit on outside while she prepared some sandwiches. He ate greedily as if he had not eaten for a long time while she watched curiously through the back door curtains. Finally he put the plate down on the greenhouse step, and leant back closing his eyes. By this time, I was watching, too, through a nearby window. His head drooped forwards in a troubled sleep and he muttered continuously. My mother was concerned that he might fall off the chair and when she went outside, realised he was speaking some strange language. Everyone was aware of the risk of invasion and spies being dropped by parachute, and I recall Uncle once assessing the number of weapons the family could muster if necessary, perhaps the pitchfork, scythe and rake. This poor mumbling stranger, slumped sideways against our coal shed door seemed harmless enough but my mother told me to go through the front door to get a neighbour, probably Mr. Bowen from next door. He agreed that the man was behaving very suspiciously, so again I was sent off to get a message to Mr. Hughes, the local constable. He often called in when passing, his friendship with my uncle dating from a night when an owl had flown at his face when he was cycling along Jack Hayes Lane. He had come in all bloody to receive first aid, and discussed the incident over a cup of tea.

The stranger was taken away in a very bewildered state, but the outcome was something we laughed about for some time. My mother's 'spy' turned out to be a missing person, an academic who had disappeared after suffering a nervous breakdown. His suspected German was either Latin or Greek. Uncle thought it was a pity that he had not been around, but approved of the action taken. I felt proud of my part in the event!

Less commendable was the amusement some of St. Chad's choristers and I expressed at an incident one Sunday. Among the curates we had at Bagnall during my childhood was a tall thin man who I believe was not very robust. He was very fair, and during the summer would put on his white surplice before leaving the parsonage to walk across the fields to church. Part of the way led through the barn fields used by a herd of long horned cattle. We had to watch where we trod but the cows did not bother us. That day a cow took exception to the striding curate, and we were all delighted to see him running for his life to finally leap a wall with his surplice billowing out around him. Someone likened him to an angel, a nickname that stuck. He was also known as the flying curate. He was a good and gentle man who despite his adventure went on to complete his parochial duties that memorable Sunday.

Some incidents can only be appreciated with the lapse of time. My mother and aunt had an experience with a chicken destined for the cooking pot. Trying to end its life as rapidly and painlessly as possible, my aunt unfortunately decapitated it. Mother who had been holding it was so shocked she let go. The headless bundle of feathers took off across the kitchen, a reflex action she had not anticipated, and where her washing, dried and ironed, hung from a rack over the stove. The mess was catastrophic, the atmosphere electric! It was the last time any animal met its end in the family kitchen. The school kitchen, serving as cloakroom and official Wardens' Post must have secretly served for this purpose from then on. The children attending the Hollies were largely unaware of such dramas that occurred behind the scenes from time to time. Not so for many of the parents. They were both supportive and encouraging, and very appreciative of all that happened, particularly when some humorous incident was shared. Most things were being done on behalf of their children!

Plate 17 *The Hollies School*

Raf, the school dog.

Raf with Lady, Phyllis Bird's border collie, the 'goatdog'.

Francis and Phyllis Bird.

Plate 19   *The Hollies School*

Shirley Coe and Sylvia Myatt, part of the 1948 Baddeley Edge troupe dancing team.

Sylvia in action.

Christine and Michael Brookes in front of Moorside, the schoolhouse.

Plate 21 *The Hollies School*

Ruth and Jeremy Francis, off to boarding school at the Hollies.

Dressed for summer in their school garden.

Out of school activities.

Playtime in the Hollies and Moorside garden.

Memories of lead soldiers, the model steam train and the school bell as it appears today.

CHAPTER 8

For some years, my aunt Phyllis had been leaving more and more of the teaching to my mother Jeanie. As the war dragged on her health deteriorated, but she was out working in the garden or tending the animals in all weathers ignoring her brother and sister's concern for her well-being. When Jean, our foster sister, left home, she seemed to lose her interest in the school. She wanted to help the young woman financially, and possibly not for the first time realised how easily she could earn a proper salary like her brother by working in a State school. My mother had always resisted any suggestion of a substantial increase in the fees, and was annoyed when I was sufficiently mature to raise the issue. Phyllis knew that their small Private School meant everything to her sister. Over the years, my mother had in fact almost made it her life. With one daughter at University and me at Grammar School, she thought of little but the welfare and education of the children in her care. Francis understood as he felt the same about his boys at Smallthorne. There must have been much discussion between the three of them and with the Education Authorities as she gradually assumed full responsibility for The Hollies. On 7th January 1947, Phyllis was appointed to Jackfields' Infant School ending, or so she thought at the time, a thirty-seven year relationship with the school founded by her mother. The change in Principal was so gradual that few children who were at the school registered this extraordinary event.

Sylvia Myatt was at The Hollies during this period of transition, from January 1944 to July 1948. She recalls, "Our teacher, Mrs. Brown, was always named Aunty Brown as she was so kind and caring; a second mother to us and indeed a lovely lady. One day during school lunch, I noticed Raffie the dog was choking. Aunty Brown immediately sorted out the problem and saved her life! Our school meals were simply delicious, home cooked by Mrs. Wilshaw. I remember the rabbit pie, and the orange jelly sponge dessert."

The orange jelly was supplied by the wartime Government to schools. It came in huge tins and was very popular, possibly because it was sweet and we never saw real oranges. Kathleen and Denis, Mrs. Wilshaw's children were entered in the school register in 1944.

Sylvia continues, "We had dancing lessons with Miss Blatchford on Wednesday afternoons. They were most enjoyable. We also practised deportment, walking around in a circle balancing a book on our heads, and the last one to retain the book won a silver sixpence. I spent many a sixpence on crayons, pencils or sweets.

Another memorable time was when we all performed on the stage at the Queen's Hall, Burslem. I was one of the fairies in a white net dress with wings. Oh! It was so exciting when we had our make-up applied. It made us so special."

"The writing lessons were with joined up letters, not printing. We were given paper or books with lines, and dots to show us where to join up each letter".

"At the back of the school there was a nice colourful garden and a few fruit bushes. One was Red Currant, bunches of them waiting to be sampled. Goats were kept at the bottom of the garden, and during break-time, we could have warmed goat's milk.

"On a table near the window of the back room in the house was a kinematograph machine which fascinated me. When a handle was turned, there were moving pictures." (This was a toy from the Victorian era, a museum piece that the children enjoyed! Sylvia also mentions a chess set dating from the same period).

"Preparing for Christmas was a busy time. We made our own cards with shiny coloured paper cut into shapes to make a picture, and a hand-written verse inside. Garlands were made from broad strips of stiff paper cut into lengths and stuck down with flour paste to make interlocking rings. The Hollies was such a friendly place, like one big happy family." Sylvia remembers Michael Jones who lived in Greasley Road, Abbey Hulton, Dr. Heard's son Juan, Norma Williams, Michael Brookes, Allen Bottomley, and her special friend Shirley Coe.

"The navy blue and red school uniform was very smart and much admired. The girls wore a navy velour brimmed hat with a red band and holly-designed badge at the front. A red-fringed girdle was worn around our tunic over a white blouse and red tie. The summer uniform was a grey blazer, a red and white cotton dress and a Panama hat. We were a credit to our parents and school".

My mother Jeanie gradually modernised the uniform, grey replacing the navy blue as children outgrew their clothing. She asked me to design a new school badge, too, and it was used from then on.

Sylvia comments on the influence the school has had on her life. She is an avid letter writer, has designed and made most of her own and her mother's clothes, is skilled in calligraphy, and sang in Church choirs and amateur Opera. She is also a keen gardener, influenced she believes by being surrounded by a lovely garden while being educated.

Edward Bottomley attended the Hollies from April 1945 to July 1951. His brother Allen was a pupil from 1942 to 1948. Edward writes, "Memories from my time at The Hollies are still vivid. Allen and I often missed the Bagnall bus with its wooden slatted seats, and had to walk up from Milton" (Upholstery could not be replaced during the war years so any new seating was similar in construction to a park bench, but less comfortable!) "The walk seemed like twenty miles! However, there were always things to do on the way, including a visit to the St. Bernard dogs at a house half way up the hill on the right hand side. Often in the Summer Allen and I would walk home across the fields to Abbey Hulton, and thence to Bucknall, getting into a few scrapes en route. Heaven knows what time we used to get to school and home again!"

"When I was six or seven, I was running around Mrs. Brown's house at playtime and fell on the ash path. A piece of barbed wire went through the palm of my right hand and out at the back. I had to be taken to the doctor at Milton to have it cut out, a big deal in those days! I was always a great hoarder and would take anything that was put down and hide it away. I got into trouble lots of times when I was caught."

Mrs. Brown had several spools of 'flip' photographs. They were put on a hand turned machine that flipped over the photographs below two magnifying glasses making the images move. We were allowed to use these on special occasions, but only if we were good. Allen and I sometimes slept over in Mrs. Brown's house and it was strange to be in such a quiet place. I remember playing at the bottom of the garden where there was a stream and an old hut. It was out of bounds but I always managed to go down there. I recall that Mrs. Brown's pupils were not allowed on the playground of Miss Bird's school. We used to watch the older students through the trees. I think our playtimes were staggered, too". (This division of the school play area must have been agreed upon in the final years before Phyllis left to teach at a State school, and is one of the few indications of changes taking place.)

Edward continues, "One day no one was allowed out at playtime as the pig that lived in a pen down the garden was to be slaughtered. To this day, I remember hearing the shot and the pig shrieking. I think we all got some pork to take home in due course". (A pig was raised annually as part of the war effort, and was mainly fed on pigswill contributed by the neighbours and parents, the meat being eventually shared. Country children in the 1940s were accustomed to such animals being slaughtered, but the first experience was a shock. I was never allowed to play with any young goats destined for the kitchen, and the calves we reared always disappeared while I was out. Rabbits met their end in my absence, too, but no one bothered about the demise of ducks or chickens!)

Edward recalls another local incident. "One lunch time an aeroplane flew very low over the school and barely missed the trees opposite. We all ran along the road and saw the pilot hanging in the trees caught by his parachute. I believe it was a German plane and it ended up nose first in the Golf Course. We managed to clamber up on it unaware of any danger".

I have very different memories of this incident. He was only five at the time and the crash was a conversational topic for many weeks. There were several plane crashes in the vicinity, two of which he could have clambered upon, but the American plane which just missed the school and the houses at the end of Jack Hayes Lane left a blazing crater in the Golf Course and the area was cordoned off. Some of the crew parachuted to safety but the pilot and another airman died in the crash.

Edward comments, "I am afraid my time at school was not the best time of my life, although I loved Mrs. Brown. Learning was difficult and I would far rather have been out fishing or gardening, anything but school! It was only after I left in 1954 that things began to click and then I could not get enough education. The grounding we got at The Hollies was excellent, pot-hooks and all!"

Bill Hassall attended The Hollies from May 1946 to July 1952. He writes,

"I was born in May, 1941, at the height of the Second World War, the only child of a farmer who ran one of the larger farms in the area. We lived approximately one mile from Miss Bird's school, the name that it was known by locally although Miss Bird no longer taught there. The only people I knew as a child apart from my parents were the three farm workers who included a Land Army girl named Sybil, and the delivery people who came to the farm. At the age of four, I was diagnosed as having TB and as a result, I spent a long time in Haywood Hospital at Burslem, the trauma of which I vividly remember to this day. When the time came for me to go to school, my parents arranged for me to go to The Hollies Private School. I was a shy boy who had not had the opportunity to mix with other children and the time in hospital had meant further isolation so there were many tears. I refused to work, and cried for much of the first half term. Mrs. Brown had to lock the school door because all I wanted was to run home. Her gentle determination won through in the end".

"I was obsessed with farming, as were many farm boys of that era, and more concerned about my own rabbits and bantams than Mrs. Brown's pothooks which one was required to complete line after line. Gradually school began to grow on me and I came to like some parts of it. I began to make friends of my own age, a good thing because I had been very much a loner. There were two great attractions, Raf the school dog who was every pupil's friend, and Miss Bird's goats who resided in sheds in a more remote part of the garden. When Mrs. Brown was not looking, we would go behind the bushes to have a look at them, even allowing the nanny goats to nibble our coat sleeves. The smell of the billy goat deterred us from close contact with him. Older children were given the job of taking Raf for a walk during the dinner hour, and one was perceived as very grown up when allowed out on this important errand. I remember on more than one occasion being late returning for lessons and not being allowed to take Raf out for the next few weeks. We soon became careful not to overrun the allotted time".

"When I started school I was taken there in the farm van used to deliver the day's milk around Light Oaks, Baddeley Edge, Milton and Baddeley Green. However, when I reached the age of seven I had to walk up the lane from the farm to Bagnall Hospital, and then across the barn fields. That barn is a ruin now and the lane has become a very busy road. I still recall certain things vividly. There was the weekly visit of Miss

Blatchford, who taught music and movement on Wednesday afternoons. On one occasion, she arranged for most if not all the pupils to perform at the Queens Theatre in Burslem. I was so scared, but somehow we performed. Many of the proud parents were amongst the audience. I remember, too, the day when we were called together following morning break to be told that the King had died and that now we had a new young Queen, Elizabeth the Second. This meant a day off on the day of the King's funeral".

"In my last year at school I and another pupil were given a very responsible job to do. This involved walking to Milton with Raf in order to take some money to the Bank. Mr. Gadd, the Manager, was telephoned and informed that we were on our way. The money was probably school fees which were payable on the first day of each new term, by then the princely sum of £3.10s. This rose to £5.00 by the time I left but I think the fees went up when a pupil reached eight".

"On another occasion I remember receiving a box of chocolates on my birthday from one of the girls. When I came to go home I found that it had been opened and the contents half eaten. The whole school was detained until the culprit was identified, and there followed the rare use of physical punishment for the crime. Looking back, I have very fond memories of Mrs. Brown, an outstanding lady to whom I owe much. She gave me such a solid educational base on which to build my life. She and my mother were two very special ladies, shining examples of truly practical and hard working Godly women. They did not have much in the way of luxuries, but gave so fully and willingly for my benefit. I would not have been where I am today if it had not been for their devotion to duty, for which I am eternally grateful".

Mary Bartlam attended The Hollies from September 1946 to July 1955, leaving at the age of fourteen to attend the Underwood Secretarial College to learn shorthand and typing before going on to work at Doulton's. She told me that she had been taught by Mrs. Brown in the house 'Moorside', and recalled when Phyllis Bird left to take charge of the Infant Class at Jackfields. She remembered, also, that later illness brought Phyllis back on the scene when she occasionally did a small amount of teaching. She still kept her goats at the back of the school, but by then a neighbour did most of the maintenance.

Both the school and the house were subsequently again used for teaching. The large schoolroom had been abandoned temporarily when my mother assumed responsibility for the entire school and Phyllis rented it briefly to a neighbour who opened a small café there. I have a dim recollection of a few tables with colourful check tablecloths, but the anticipated customers from the hourly bus did not materialise and the venture failed. At some later date, my mother had a third of the room overlooking the greenhouse and garden partitioned off. This provided an area for her assistant, Norma Williams, to teach small groups of children and shows that my aunt was still taking some interest in the school. She owned the building so had to consent to the structural alteration, something that must have been discussed with her brother and sister. Norma had entered The Hollies in March 1944 when she was $8^1/_2$ and seems to have stayed on to become a highly regarded and responsible pupil teacher.

Mary also recalls a Mrs. Glover then employed as school cook, and Masie Blatchford "who taught us to dance and made us walk with books on our heads". Once again, the school dog Raf featured among her happy memories. "We used to take the black dog Raf for walks on the Golf Links at dinnertime to meet the children who had gone home coming back". Mary mentioned a number of her school companions, William Hassell, Mary Warner, Michael Berrisford, Susan Key, Robert and Carol Brown, John and Kathleen Brown, Brian Birch, Shirley Coe, Allen and Edward Bottomley, Michael and Christine Brookes, and Kathleen Potts.

By the time Mary left The Hollies I was in my mid twenties and living in London. I was more aware of what was going on at Light Oaks than I had been for some years. My own two children were now boarders, and though their absence through each school term left a great gap in my life, I knew they were safe and in loving hands, and that their lives would be an ongoing educational experience just as mine had been. Francis continued to organise day excursions and holidays almost to the end of his life.

David Heath of Audley wrote to me as follows: "I once visited the school around 1957. At that time, I was a pupil at Smallthorne County Primary school and one of my teachers was a Mr. Bird, an elderly gentleman who had also taught my father around 1919. He had been in the Navy before entering the teaching profession. Mr. Bird was a wonderful character and was an enthusiastic youth hosteller. I remember him taking groups of pupils on various treks staying at different Youth Hostels. On one occasion, I visited Mr. Bird for tea at The Hollies. The lady there I believe was his sister Jeanie. I have very happy memories of that time". Youth hostelling was an economical way to travel, providing opportunities to visit historic sites, museums and areas of geological interest. Before leaving home, I had shared a number of such trips with my uncle, and in later years, my children would enjoy many such excursions with their great uncle Francis.

CHAPTER 9

Michael Brookes attended The Hollies from April 1947 to July 1954. He remembered that it was at the time the school was run by Mrs. Jeanie Brown. "She was a truly remarkable woman", he writes, "and I have often reflected on the years that I experienced her teaching and guidance and marvelled at the enormity of the task she undertook. Not only did she educate twenty or more children of different ages and abilities all at one time, quite a feat in itself, but she also managed to write and produce school plays and conduct daily worship with the singing of a hymn. Amazingly she provided a hot dinner and pudding for us all every day, too".

"I think that towards the end of my time at the school she did have some help from Norma Williams who was only in her teens. Norma was able to hear us read and, I remember, taught us how to look up a hymn number and find words in a dictionary".

"Once a week we had a visit from a dance teacher, Miss Blatchford, but the word 'dance' is misleading. We seemed to do things that would equate more to modern aerobics than dancing! We also had a weekly elocution lesson from Mrs. Doreen Malbon who came on a peripatetic basis. The only other contributor to the smooth running of the enterprise was a Mrs. Steele who lived almost opposite the school and helped with the cooking and cleaning".

"The BBC used to broadcast programmes for schools, and Mrs. Brown made use of these. She sent for the published booklets that went with the programmes and we would all participate as William Appleby taught us folk songs from all over the world in a programme called 'Singing Together'. A similar programme was 'Music and Movement' where we all moved about pretending to be birds, butterflies or giants".

"Mrs. Brown had a vivid imagination and would write fantastic stories about dragons and other mythical creatures. When she read them to us, the whole school was wide-eyed with suspense and wonderment. Her school plays varied in their subject and were ambitious. I remember one where we were dressed as flowers with names like Daffi-down-dilly. A

73

play that stands out in my memory was performed at the end of the Autumn Term. It involved a Narrator, the part spoken by me, but the main character was Father Christmas, played by Brian Birch. We rehearsed for many weeks. A few days before the performance Mrs. Brown walked into the classroom with a grim face and said "Children, the play is off"! Brian Birch had contracted mumps and there was nobody to take on the role of the main character unless, and she looked at me. Because I was timid I had been given the smallest part, but I was the only one who was not on stage at the same time as Father Christmas. What choice did I have? Needless to say, I had to agree and the production was saved. My mother hurriedly sewed together a 'Santa suit' and the play was declared a great success. My proudest moment was when Mrs. Brown told the audience how I had saved the day and I was given a special round of applause".

"Playtimes hold some special memories. We had the free run of most of the garden. It had a concrete square where we played games such as 'Puss Puss', 'May I' and 'Letters in your Name'. One side of the square led to secret paths where we played hide and seek. There was one particularly large tree that all the boys loved to climb. I shudder to think what the next-door neighbour, Mrs. Bowen, must have endured as twenty boisterous children were let loose twice a day! Part of the garden was out of bounds and contained sheds where Miss Bird kept goats. We were a little afraid of these smelly creatures with their fierce looking horns so only the bravest were tempted to stray down the forbidden path".

"Mrs. Brown's dog Raf was a great favourite with the children. When we were in our final year (10 or 11 years old), two or three of us were allowed to take her for walks. We invariably made for the nearby Greenway Hall Golf Course. Many a happy hour was spent wandering over the fairways and playing in the stream that ran along the far boundary. Raf was a bitch and Mrs. Brown was careful to keep her indoors when she was in season. On one occasion however, she escaped and was 'molested' by the neighbourhood Romeo on the front lawn of the school. We children stood around in rapt amazement as Mrs. Brown frantically beat both dogs with a walking stick in an effort to separate them. We wide-eyed innocents did not understand the significance of what was going on and Mrs. Brown made no attempt to explain, preferring to draw a discrete veil over the event".

"Occasions that needed a firm disciplinary hand were few and far between, but when such events did occur, the miscreants were dealt with swiftly, receiving a sound smacking. There was one boy (isn't there always?) who seemed to need this more than most and on one occasion after nursing a smarting bottom he stood up filled with remorse saying "I'll dead myself" over and over again".

"I was not only timid but small for my age and quite puny. This gave me something of an inferiority complex and Mrs. Brown was aware of this. She would encourage me saying, 'Try to be bolder! Remember that you're as good as most and better than some!' This little saying has stood me in good stead throughout my life. I remember an occasion when a boy who was a similar age to me but much bigger physically, complained to his father that I had been bullying him. His father came to the school and spoke to Mrs. Brown about it. Puzzled, she sent for me and when the father saw me standing next to his son he beat a hasty and embarrassed retreat".

"Childhood's formative years and the experiences and lessons learned affect the whole of our lives. I will always be grateful for the start that my sister and I received at The Hollies and the excellent all round education given by the dedication and enthusiasm of Mrs. Jeanie Brown".

Christine Clipson (nee Brookes), Michael's sister, was at The Hollies from September 1949 to July 1955. "I started at The Hollies when I was four years old", she told me. "The fees were £4.10 shillings per term. My brother, a year and a half older, was such a cry baby that he would not go to school alone, so I was allowed to go with him to keep him company. I continued there until I took my eleven plus exam and went on to Brownhills High School".

"Mrs. Brown was the most wonderful teacher. She was strict but never frightening. She kept us in order with an occasional slap across the legs with a ruler to discourage laziness, but mostly she was kind, understanding, and tremendous fun. I remember her as a very old lady, although she was only fifty, with her grey hair tied back in a bun, a mole on her nose and thick grey stockings darned at the knees in different colours".

"When I first went to school Norma Williams, her assistant, taught the younger children in the 'Morning Room'. Norma was a gentle girl in delicate health. I remember her patiently helping me to unravel the mysteries of tens and units with the help of coloured wooden counters. She also introduced me to the first Beacon Reader cards, printed in black and red with sentences such as "The little red hen went into the farmyard".

"The schoolroom was in the main living area of the house and consisted of the front and back rooms knocked into one. We had our lunch there, did our morning exercises, had morning prayers and enjoyed the BBC's 'Music and Movement' classes. It must have involved a lot of furniture moving! Sometime after the death of King George VI, the school moved next door into Miss Bird's house. The day he died, we were enjoying Music and Movement, jumping about being gnomes and fairies, when the wireless went suddenly quiet. Then a chilling voice announced that the King was dead. It seemed like weeks to me before the BBC stopped playing that awful mournful dirge and we had our lovely school broadcasts back again. What joy to be 'Singing Together' with William Appleby!".

"The only time we went upstairs in Mrs. Brown's house was to visit the lavatory and occasionally to listen to an educational broadcast in the front sitting room. The back bedroom fascinated us. This was the private domain of Francis Bird, known affectionately as 'Uncle's Wubbish Woom', a name coined by Ruth Francis, Mrs. Brown's granddaughter", (a boarder at the school from April 1954 to July 1959). "The room was always kept locked away from prying young eyes and we would speculate often on what wonders it might hold. Only once did I get a glimpse inside and the memory will remain with me always. I had gone to the bathroom and Uncle's door was open. Rooted to the spot, I stared wide eyed at the amazing collection of books, papers, pieces of coral, antique instruments and strange and wonderful souvenirs of his travels. Then Mrs. Brown appeared and hustled me swiftly down the stairs".

"I think it was probably in my last year that we moved next door. Phyllis Bird came back to join Mrs. Brown in the school. They had two separate classrooms. Miss Bird took the children preparing for eleven-plus, including myself. Mrs. Brown took the younger children in the larger classroom at the front. My most vivid memories of school are of the earlier times in Mrs. Brown's house".

"I can still see the playground and garden clearly, and the covered porch at the back with a very smelly lavatory and pipes that always froze in winter. Steps down from the porch divided a rockery and gave onto a square of concrete known as the 'Cement'. This was our main play area, together with a path that led under Mrs. Brown's kitchen window and around to the front of the two buildings. The most exciting part was the garden beyond the Cement. It seemed to go on for miles with overgrown pathways and tunnels under the bushes made by former pupils. It was great for adventure games, especially when Mrs. Brown had read a book to us about the Amazon jungle with boa constrictors and creepers that twined themselves around people. Oh! The delicious fear as we crawled through the undergrowth searching for the great river Amazon. The only animals we found were the goats and rabbits, kept in sheds at the bottom of the garden"!

"Winter seems to loom large in my recollections of The Hollies. When it snowed, the bus could not get up the hill from Milton to collect us and we had to walk down to meet our parents at the bottom. It was great fun. On one occasion the bus had tried to get up but skidded and became wedged sideways across the road. There was no room to walk around it so the emergency door was opened and we were lifted inside to cross the gangway to get out through the passenger door. Our schoolroom was heated with a coal fire at one end and on winter afternoons, we sat in a group around the fire while Mrs. Brown told us wonderful stories. My brother Michael, and Michael Beresford and Brian Birch took turns at being 'Minister for Fuel and Power' with the huge responsibility of keeping the fire going. (Michael Beresford and Brian Birch both came to The Hollies in April 1948.) Often when the weather was bad, there was a power cut and the room was lit with candles, a perfect atmosphere for storytelling. I remember that Mrs. Brown wrote books for children".

My mother wrote two children's books 'Smoke Beneath the Flagstones' and 'The Three P's at Valley Farm', published by Newnes in the early 1940s. Unfortunately, her many other children's stories and novels were never offered to a publisher. Christine recalls a dusty, typed manuscript left on a windowsill with the intriguing title "Dogged by Dogs" by Jeanie Brown. She says. "I always longed to read it but never dared to ask. One story she told us was about a woman whose hair kept growing longer and longer until it filled the room and she couldn't breathe. It was really frightening. Some of her favourite stories were the Greek myths, especially the tales of Odysseus and his years of voyaging around the Aegean. She pronounced his name as O-dus-seus and it was not until I was an adult that I realised Odysseus was the same person! She really brought the characters to life. I particularly liked Polyphemus with his one eye".

She also told us a lot about her own life. She must have lived in Queensland, Australia. She said that she and the children ran barefoot and jiggers burrowed into the soles of their feet and had to be dug out. She liked to tell us scary or unpleasant things. I think she enjoyed the expressions of horror on our faces. She also talked about Canada sometimes". My mother was obviously blending fact and fiction for the children's entertainment and education. I found it interesting that she could refer to Canada at this stage in her life, something she had never been able to do when I was a child.

Christine refers to the Christmas plays when parents came up to school to watch the children perform. She says, "Mrs. Brown wrote the scripts. I remember standing centre stage to deliver some opening lines, 'I'm going on a long journey, all the way to London on a bus. Daddy says I'll fall asleep and dream of chalk and cheese!' The rest of the play was the dream itself giving great scope for her lively imagination".

"Mrs. Steele, a neighbour, used to come in to cook the lunches and do the cleaning. One day she did not come any more and Mrs. Brown took on the job of cooking our meals. The meals were wonderful, steak and kidney puddings, Spotted Dick and custard or jam roly-poly. How on earth did she manage to teach us and feed us without completely losing her sense of humour? I was a difficult child at first when it came to eating. I would sit for ages over a bowl of custard and often refused to eat at all. Mrs. Brown put a chair piled high with books next to me at the table. She sat my teddy bear on the top and gave him a plate of custard, too. That solved the problem."

"I remember once finding a Pound note behind the wall at the end of the lane while we were waiting for the bus. My mother came with me to the police station to hand it in and we were told that if nobody claimed it within six months I could come and collect it. It seemed a wait of a lifetime but I finally got my Pound. What a lot of money it was then! The bus rides up and down the hill to Milton were an important part of our day and the only time we were not supervised, a situation of which we took full advantage. If anyone behaved too badly the conductor would hoist the culprit up on to the luggage rack and leave him or her there for the rest of the journey. As we spilled off the bus at the end of Jack Hayes Lane in the mornings, the children for Bagnall School would be waiting to board. They would jeer at us, call us names and laugh at our uniforms. They called me 'Freckles' which I took as a serious insult, although it was apt".

"In my last term at The Hollies Mrs. Brown and Miss Bird took the whole school on a summer picnic to Trentham Park. Raf, the black spaniel/setter cross came, too. We went by the ordinary service bus, changing buses in Hanley. Our picnic was on the banks of a stream. Afterwards we were allowed to paddle and search for wildlife. I remember we girls wore our red gingham dresses tucked into our knickers, bottoms up in the air, looking for sticklebacks. Another excursion was to Wetley Common with Miss Bird. It was part of our Nature Study course. We collected many types of different grasses and took them back to school to draw in our nature books". My aunt spent many hours meticulously making small pastel sketches of plants and aquatic life, and had always encouraged this activity in school.

Christine ends her reminiscences with this comment. "Children tend to accept things at face value and it never occurred to me to wonder how long Mrs. Brown had been at The Hollies or how the school began. I owe her such a debt of gratitude for the enormous breadth of education she gave me. Even at University, I would sometimes come up with an obscure piece of knowledge that no one else seemed to have been taught. She instilled a set of values that I have always tried to retain. The principle of racial equality was drummed into us so firmly that even now I react vehemently when someone shows racism. What a huge influence she had on my life".

Christine listed the names of pupils she remembers roughly in age sequence beginning with the eldest, but siblings have been placed together for ease of reference.

Edward Bottomley *(son of the Vicar of Bucknall)*
John Horden *(Mum was a District Nurse)*
Bill Hassall *(Family were farmers)*
Reggie, John and David Ash
Michael Brookes *(my brother)*
Michael Beresford *(The family had a Bakery in Bucknall)*
Brian Birch *(Birch's Shoe Repairs, Hanley)*
Mary Bartlam *(Farmers in the Bucknall area)*
Melvin Grocott *(local to Light Oaks)*
Michael Challener *(local to Light Oaks)*
Christine Brookes *(myself)*
Carol Chapell *(Family lived at Milton)*
Ann and Sally Mulrennan *(Father was Vicar of Abbey Hulton)*
Kathleen Potts *(a boarder at the Hollies, daughter of Phyllis Bird's foster child)*
Susan Capey *(local to Light Oaks)*
Susan Key *(local to Light Oaks)*
Carol and John Brown *(local to Light Oaks)*
Michael Bratt *(Family lived in Hanley)*
Ruth and Jeremy Francis *(boarders at The Hollies and Jeanie Brown's grand- children)*
Barry and Larry Keeling *(Adopted sons of a family from Waterhouses, red haired, freckled and pure dynamite)*
Michael Harper *(Father had a Pharmacy in Abbey Hulton)*
Christopher Cunningham *(neighbours of the Harpers)*
Yvonne Le Rolland *(I think they had an oatcake shop in Milton)*
David and Judith Vincent
David Ruffles and a brother, possibly John.

Quite a feat of memory on Christine's part!

CHAPTER 10

Jeremy Francis attended The Hollies as a boarder from September 1954 to July 1959.

He first recalls the large wooden board nailed to the huge Sycamore tree proclaiming the existence of The Hollies Private School. "The Hollies was a very special sort of private school", he writes, "though not in the sense that it catered for an elite and groomed young prodigies. In fact, it was almost the opposite. Mrs. Brown, whom in my day was the headmistress and proprietor, had an open door policy. Children were admitted from across the board and more than one of my contemporaries enjoyed her generous support when the minimal and modest school fees were beyond the means of the families, or not forthcoming from other sources".

"Few, if any of those who attended the school would ever forget the indefatigable Mrs. Brown, or indeed the formidable Miss Bird, a strict disciplinarian who ruled with an iron hand, or rather with a twelve inch ruler that was quick to make an appearance in the event of sloppy work or insubordination of any kind".

"For most, the sound of the school bell signalling the end of playtime or the call for lunch must be etched in their memories forever. To be allowed to perform this duty was an accolade of the first order and a cherished privilege. It imbued a special sort of status on the bell ringer and a careful sense of timing as a second too early would cut short playtime and a second too late would incur the wrath of Miss Bird, a stickler for punctuality".

"Several of the pupils lived in the immediate vicinity, but most arrived on the hourly bus which disgorged its load at the end of Jack Hayes Lane at a few minutes to nine each morning en route for Bagnall. One or two of the children had parents who owned cars and with the arrival of each car more pupils would spill out until suddenly the school was full and the serious business of the day commenced. Reading, writing and arithmetic, a school curriculum second to none. On certain days, the wireless was carefully tuned to the BBC school programme and we would spend many happy hours engrossed in music and movement, pretending to be trees or opening flowers, or occasionally playact being fast asleep which was always very popular. On other occasions, Mrs. Malbon would arrive to give us elocution lessons and prepare us vigorously for the poetry competitions. The school had an enviable track record, often claiming top prizes at the North Staffordshire Music and Poetry festivals".

"Swimming was a special treat involving a bus to Hanley and the PMT bus to Newcastle-under-Lyme where we had weekly lessons at the public baths. Mrs. Brown, by this time well into her fifties, learnt to dive along with the rest of us, stoutly maintaining that it was not the prerogative of youth. For many of the children, I am sure that learning to swim has remained a life long pleasure. Some of the pupils were able to visit the riding school at Abbey Hulton, too, which I believe still exists and was run by the same family not many years ago".

"The piano teacher gave us lessons in her own home at the bottom of the hill, a very kind lady with a frightfully grand Rover car in the drive. Raf and Lady, the two school dogs, would appear at the gate when we returned on the bus. Such happy days!"

"From time to time Mrs. Brown would take us to the Doctor at Milton for vaccinations. These were administered with huge syringes and seemingly, absolutely enormous needles which I remember as being extremely painful. On the way back we would visit Barclays Bank on the corner that now appears to me to have had the same sort of atmosphere as a funeral home. Banks were very serious places in those days, especially for small children. Mrs. Brown would give us a few coins and we would cross the road to the Oat Cake shop owned by David's dad and buy some oatcakes to take home. David LeRolland was one of my friends and a fellow pupil at school".

"Occasionally Mrs. Brown would appear visibly worried and Miss Bird would fret for days on end until the impending visit of the school inspector had passed. A few days later an official brown envelope from the education department would arrive, giving the school a glowing report. Beaming parents would congratulate the headmistress and even the school bell would seem to have something a little extra in its cheerful ring".

"Mrs. Steele came in each morning and busied herself in the kitchen. Mrs. Brown, also busy as always, would dash out of class to supervise the cooking of the school lunch, which was plentiful and always delicious, Mrs. Brown often feigning a lack of appetite to make a little bit extra for those of us who still felt hungry. The puddings were, Oh! so good! Steamed treacle puddings and custard, spotted dick, or rhubarb from Miss Bird's garden. Few could have complained about the food. Salt in those days was supplied in large blocks wrapped in greaseproof paper, and one of my special tasks was to grind this up and store it in the large sweet jars kept for the purpose. It was always a task one made to last as long as possible and a source of endless pleasure for my young imagination as I carved tunnels and caves, roads and bridges, and mountains and valleys among other themes before Mrs. Brown would gently insist that the task had taken too long. Occasionally we were allowed to operate the potato peeler, a magnificent gadget that attached to the cold-water tap and rotated under the pressure of the water, peeling the contents in the process. Less favoured were dishwashing duties, but I am sure we all did our fair share. Woes betide any unfortunate spider that found its way into the kitchen. The otherwise saintly Mrs. Brown would swiftly despatch the errant creature, consigning it to the flames of the Rayburn cooker that glowed night and day. The dough for her homemade bread was frequently rising behind the hot plates and the huge pans of hot water steaming in readiness for lunch".

"The commercial traveller who used to arrive from time to time was a more welcome visitor to the kitchen. A few days later a van would deliver new supplies for the pantry and the school tuck shop, always a favourite. Blackjacks and smarties, farthing chews and on one occasion aniseed balls. Mrs. Brown never inflated the prices and remembering her as I do, I would not be surprised if she did not subsidise the whole enterprise. Only certain sweets were approved, however. Iced lollies were definitely off the agenda and ice cream unthinkable if eaten in public! Nobody would have considered the school snobbish, but there was a certain cachet associated with being one of the children at The Hollies. As such, we had to be on our best behaviour especially on school outings and trips into town. The bus to Hanley passed the cemetery and crematorium at Abbey Hulton and would frequently have to slow down or stop for a passing funeral cortege. Pupils from The

Hollies would doff their caps in respect. Children from other schools rarely bothered".

"No school term would have been complete without a visit to the dentist, whom we were all convinced had been part of Hitler's war time programme before being let loose on local children. A loose tooth would be handled by Mrs. Brown. She would attach a cord to a door handle, the other end around the offending tooth, before swiftly closing the door to remove the problem. I am sure, whatever else may have changed since those days, children have been given a more positive view of dental care".

"Playtime was always special. One boy, Joseph Pickering, had an imaginary lorry that remained parked in the playground. He drove it every day, meticulously accelerating through the gears and slowing to a halt before reversing carefully into the allocated parking space as the school bell indicated time was up. He must have covered hundreds of miles each term, and I am sure when he left school must have gone on to be a transport magnate of some kind. Whilst Joseph drove his truck, one or two of the girls would exchange notes and play doctors and nurses with the older boys in the outside toilet. Although it was a perfectly innocent activity, it certainly was not part of the school schedule, but nevertheless provided invaluable sex education for youthful minds".

"We rarely played ball games. This may account for my singular lack of interest as an adult. I do not believe the school numbered any famous footballers amongst the former pupils. We frequently climbed the larch tree planted by my mother, a former pupil at the school, until the summons of the bell would end our skywards expeditions. The tree stood outside Mr. Bird's room. That upstairs room was always a source of wonderment on my frequent visits. Every corner was occupied with endless treasures such as snakes and slow worms preserved in formaldehyde. A gas mask and helmet were wartime relics, letters and papers piled to the ceiling, and a wonderful stamp collection. There were beasts mounted on plaques, trophies from some hunting trip. A carved wooden chest was full of ecclesiastical Stoles and embroidered altar cloths inherited from his father, the former curate of the parish. Most spectacular of all was a working model steam engine that his father had built, with several bits of rolling stock and all the lines, and a collection of cast lead soldiers, some of them mounted on horse back. Sometimes we would set out the rails in the garden and send the engine chugging away loaded with soldiers going off to do imaginary battle. If any of the enemy were caught, they were instantly laid on the rails and occasionally decapitated by the engine on its next appearance. Children's toys of yesterday are invaluable collectors' items today!"

There were a number of soldiers and horses that had lost their heads through age, not wilful destruction! The broken parts were put together with bits of matchstick, and were allowed in my childhood to be used as targets for Uncle's replica field guns that could shoot a darning needle accurately for several feet.

"Mr. Bird did not teach at The Hollies as he held a teaching position elsewhere, but he was frequently involved in school productions and activities. I recall that on one occasion, having been cast in some minor role, I was struck with stage fright minutes before all the parents were due to arrive. Mr. Bird and Stella Sant's dad had to climb a ladder to coax me from the upstairs bathroom where I had taken flight and locked the door, refusing all entreaties to make an appearance. Mr. Bird used to light the fireworks for the school party on November 5th, sending rockets zooming overhead, and Catherine wheels that he had nailed to the big Sycamore tree spinning madly in the early autumn night. The budget was always modest but the results marvellous".

"A collection of scientifically prepared microscopic slides was one of the mainstays of the science department. Nowadays people would throw up their hands in horror that young children were allowed to handle such things. Miss Bird was in charge of science, and we would often be allowed into her greenhouse behind the schoolroom to admire her chrysanthemums and geraniums, always a treat".

"Sometimes we would accompany Mrs. Brown to Stoke or Longton to buy school supplies, blackboard chalks, dusters and the like. On one of these trips, we acquired a little pink table and chairs for the infants, and I remember sitting at this on many occasions. For reasons that I cannot now recall Mrs. Brown was sleeping downstairs on a mattress", (probably having given up her own bed to visitors!) "When part of the ceiling collapsed. The table intercepted the falling plaster, possibly saving her life. The little pink table was even more highly prized after that event!"

The plaster was the original ceiling, dating from the early 1930s, and had no doubt been cracked and weakened by the continuous heavy use of the upstairs front room that had recently been converted into two bedrooms. The downstairs schoolroom ceiling was replaced by plasterboard that would not collapse in the heavy jagged pieces of the material formerly used in house construction.

Jeremy continues, "The school holidays would see my sister Ruth and I return to our Mother's home in London often accompanied by Mrs. Brown for some if not all of the time. These trips were always great events and we would eagerly await the arrival of the Stafford bound train where we would change and board a train to Euston. The train journey used to take six hours, but on one occasion was considerably longer due to an accident just outside Tamworth. A huge black steam engine lay on its side with coaches skewed across the track as we crept slowly past. We later learnt that there had been many fatalities. I cannot recall details but it must have made a very profound impression on my young mind as I can still picture the scene today. The rest of the journey was very subdued".

"From time to time Mrs. Brown would take my sister and I to the cinema in Hanley. Few of the films that we saw have remained with me, but I do remember having to be taken out half way through 'A Tale of Two Cities' set in the period of the French revolution. I was terrified as heads started to roll beneath the swishing blade of the Guillotine. It was many years before my sister stopped reminding me that she had been brave enough to stay and watch the rest of the film".

"After most of the other children had gone home on the four o'clock bus my sister and I would do our homework whilst Mrs. Brown prepared supper. During school time, we were always treated very formally and it is probably true to say on occasion more harshly than some of the other children, to make absolutely sure we were not considered to be 'teacher's favourite'. But after school the atmosphere became less formal. Miss Bird, our Great Aunt, would revert to being Auntie Billy, a nickname she had acquired during the First World War when she started keeping goats to supplement the family food supply. Mrs. Brown, Billy's sister and our Grandmother, would become Grannie, and Mr. Bird, their older brother, Uncle Frank".

"On Sunday morning, my sister and I would walk across the fields to St. Chad's at Bagnall, hoping to arrive at the church after Auntie Billy who usually took the bus. This enabled us to sit in a pew at the back of the church and roll marbles up and down the groove on the ledge for prayer and hymnbooks. On one occasion our activity did not go unnoticed and the vicar paused in the delivery of his sermon as a result of a wayward marble that spun out of the groove and went bouncing off on a journey of its own down the aisle. The entire congregation turned to see what had caused the commotion, all eyes seeming to focus on a very red-faced culprit. Although it cannot be said very often, especially of churches, I would have been glad for the floor to have opened up and swallowed me".

"Auntie Billy was in the habit of going into town on Saturdays. Her schedule was usually fairly precise, always returning on the same bus. On one memorable Saturday, she did not return. Several hours later, my Grandmother was frantic with worry, and called the North Staffordshire Infirmary. She learnt that Auntie Billy had collapsed in Hanley with a severe heart attack. Some time later she was able to return home and eventually resumed some of her teaching duties. I do not know how my Grandmother coped, as she not only continued to run the school somehow making time for extra classes, but also nursed Auntie Billy back to health and helped her through her convalescence. For the record both of them lived well into their eighties".

"Raf, my mother's dog and constant childhood companion before she became the School dog, finally reached the age of sixteen and a half. She would lie in front of the stove or in her box beneath the stairs sleeping the hours away, but was no longer well. One of the saddest days of my life was hearing the shot from a local farmer's gun when Granny eventually and most reluctantly decided Raf had become too old to carry on".

"The model steam engine, the lead soldiers and most of Uncle's stamps remain in my possession to this day, and in case any former pupil or elderly resident of Light Oaks wonders what happened to the school bell of all those years ago, it now hangs in my garden in Mallorca where

I have made my home. I still thrill to its sound that evokes so many happy memories of The Hollies Private School, which for much of my childhood was also my home".

Plate 25   *The Hollies School*

The rear of the Hollies showing the flat roof of the main school, greenhouse and shelter.

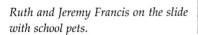

Ruth and Jeremy Francis on the slide with school pets.

A rear view of Moorside.

Saturday riding for boarders.

Plate 27   *The Hollies School*

Ruth Francis rehearsing for a school play.

Jeanie Brown, Headteacher with her sister Phyllis Bird.

Heather Norris in the uniform of the 1960s outside school and at the end of a school day.

Plate 29   *The Hollies School*

Unchecked vegetation turned the house and school gardens into an adventure playground.

Alice in Wonderland, another successful school play.

Plate 31   *The Hollies School*

Recent views of St. Chads, Bagnall and the old Butter Cross.

Moorside (below) and the Hollies School (above) as they appear today.

CHAPTER 11

Heather Norris Nicholson (nee Norris) attended The Hollies from the spring of 1964 to July 1968. She writes,

"Digging back to memories of attending school between the ages of seven and ten is a curious process. The following may or may not be how it seemed to others who recall the same period but this is how it now seems to me, looking back at those years from a height of roughly four feet, two and three quarter inches.

I attended The Hollies between 1964 and 1968, taking the eleven plus exam when I was ten and moving on to the Orme Girls' School. Did the school close when I left? Presumably, the eight or so remaining pupils all felt the same way that we were so indispensable the school couldn't carry on without us. Little did I, at least, then appreciate the commitment and sheer stamina that Mrs Brown and Miss Bird must have had in continuing to teach until their respective ages of sixty-nine and seventy-three years.

Going to school involved travelling on three smoky buses across the Potteries and often a long walk from Milton to Light Oakes. Buses and bus stops were cold until I received some woolly tights more widely available abroad than in England during the sixties. There were two kinds of bus seats, those with scratchy short carpet pile and those of smooth green leatherette that made excellent slides and could hold up to eight adults who would cling together as we all lurched around corners. Tickets from the Potteries Motor Traction bus company were also long and green. They could be made into excellent concertinas as I gazed at other passengers or the world beyond the steamed up windows. Corner shops and terraces of red brick houses, slag heaps, bottle ovens, housing estates, billboards promoting The Sound of Music and the occasional rag and bone cart carrying scrap metal were all part of the daily journey to school. So too were the women with pink and yellow hair curlers poking out from under head-scarves or plastic rain hats, and the "Don't Spit" notices on the buses where conductors sometimes sang and tried to make the passengers laugh.

I remember reading on the journeys, too, but have no sense of doing homework on the bus until going to secondary school. Bags remain clear in my mind; for reaching the upper deck was quite a struggle with bags for weekly piano lessons and Wednesday afternoon trips to the swimming baths at Newcastle-under-Lyme where a rubber ring helped Mrs Brown teach me to swim and wagon wheels or crisps with salt in twists of blue paper helped me home. Survival tips for travelling took other forms, too: Did I really reject that many strangers trying to offer me poisoned sweets? Did so many drivers, claiming to be family friends, find themselves shunned by a plodding child in grey? It seems so now.

School itself is rather a blur. Strictness prevailed with no concessions for being a member of the family. The dreaded brussels sprouts, stewed rhubarb or gooseberries deprived me of many playtimes. My debut as a protestor did not go down well either. Our reasons for chanting and marching around the school have long since faded but Iris Wood's displeasure, Mrs Brown's ire and the further loss of 'break' remain very clear. Serious anti-social behaviour did occur, not least because of the school's commitment to take in pupils who had not flourished elsewhere. In the days when shiny Izal still dominated, Mrs Brown's decadent use of soft tissue paper with Polyfilla to plug the holes that were gouged repeatedly in the classroom wall is indicative of the determination to offer all children, even the unruly ones, the chance to learn. Perhaps it hinted, too, of the self-help ethos that both sisters brought to the school from an earlier generation. Other clues included the tumble down goat sheds once used to rear animals for school dinners during the Second World War and the individual desks made for children of different sizes. Recycling and improvisation were all part of the process of teaching and learning; although I think then I just felt some things were ancient.

Some books were very old indeed. One maths book was dated 1899 and required calculations about the length of time it took different numbers of men to lay hedges, dig ditches and carry sacks of coal. At least I saw coal lorries regularly. By comparison, Beacon books, dating from the 1940s, seemed quite exciting: the dial on a wireless set and a recipe for fudge introduced exercises on fractions; a transatlantic flying boat introduced weights and times! Even then I rarely gained the large curly R (for being right?) that was part of Miss Bird's inimitable marking style. Some new books persisted with very old ideas: we practised handwriting skills in wide copybooks published by Ginn and bought from Webberley's in Hanley.

Everyday we all took turns to read aloud. Tales of adventure set in distant times and places effortlessly fulfiled the needs of today's literacy hour. Children's names are jotted down in Mrs Brown's handwriting in the margins of my surviving copy of Cynthia Harnett's *The Woolpack*. Where the names cease indicates the start of the most enjoyable part - hearing the story come alive through Mrs Brown's imaginative reading aloud. Colin, Colin, Paula, Howard, John, Gary, Frances and Jane - I wonder where they are now?

Nature study was another highlight: we tackled remarkably detailed drawings of animals, birds, flowers and seashells using fine pencil crayons. Under Miss Bird's beady-eyed supervision, we traced outlines from books and then coloured them in following clues in the text accompanying black and white pictures. As we made our simple drawings using expensive crayons purchased at Webberley's from display racks like grounded rainbows, we little knew how much knowledge of natural history guided those strict instructions about fur, fins and feathers. I do recall Miss Bird's own deft drawings but only later did I recognise their quality. She illustrated her own field notebooks with meticulously annotated sketches and added drawings to supplement or, in places, rectify artists' impressions in published works. The delicate pencil strokes on soft cartridge paper still convey her appreciation for the wonder of the natural world.

Some lessons took place outside: we used to sit in a circle under a large conifer half way down the garden. Did the desks sometimes come out onto the Cement? This was a hard surfaced area that lay between the kitchen, the no go areas of Miss Bird's amazing garden and the Shelter, a lean-to building that adjoined the original school building and where we used to play on rainy days. A bowl of tadpoles turned into frogs unexpectedly quickly and escaped from the Shelter one spring. We also played terrible duets and renderings of Chopsticks on an upright piano that spent time there before its untimely end. For the most part, formal teaching was indoors, even when we later found some larvae in stagnant water that seemed just like the mosquito cycle we had just traced as part of a lesson upstairs on locks and the building of the Panama Canal.

Outside was fantastic for break-time. We played a tag game called Relieve-0 that involved rescuing stranded players by diving through their legs. Tick was an even simpler version of tag and we evaded 'It' by running in the rougher parts of the garden, too. Crossing the River involved leaping across the cement garden path without being caught by a crocodile. The greater hazard was trying not to fall on cinders that were tipped out regularly from the kitchen Aga or the hearths to reduce the stickiness of the clayey ground. On wet days, we were restricted to the Shelter where we played such games as Grandmother's Footsteps and What's the Time, Mr Wolf? Later we played a variety of quiz games that linked our progression towards the winning post with our skills in naming food, countries, pop stars and so on in response to different letters called out by 'It'. A dank and dark toilet gave its own distinctive smell to this play-space so other parts of the garden were infinitely more interesting.

I remember some outdoor activities very clearly. We dug deep pits and channels to expose clay for making pots and different types of crockery. Our excavations and elaborate water drainage systems must have been very hazardous when washing was pegged out to dry. Tunnels through dense bushes provided exciting hiding places and escape routes. Tall trees became ships, castles and elevated route-ways for more daring kinds of tag. We built huts using fallen branches and gathered armfuls of grass for thatching. The ideal hut would have a look out tree accessed from inside the structure and barriers to keep away intruders. When building supplies ran out, we crawled into the overgrown garden next door and snaked our way along, triumphant in our double crime of theft and trespass as we returned with huge bundles of long stemmed grass that gradually turned from green to gold then soggy brown. I've now forgotten the precise function of our huts and how we decided who was inside and outside but they were a distinctive part of being at the Hollies and they did not seem to bother any adults, although where all the branches came from I can't imagine.

I remember spending some lunch times indoors and that was how the plays came about. On the bookshelves were collections of short one-act play scripts and other play-texts that dated from the time when the two sisters' brother, Francis Bird, had been an active member of an amateur drama club. We became involved in reading them aloud and then trying to walk through simple performances, reading our lines from the small blue books. The plays seemed stilted and old fashioned and then someone suggested that we should perform Alice in Wonderland. We converted downstairs into a theatre, the folding white doors defining the acting area and where our audience would sit. The set consisted of a washing line hung with old grey army blankets, a folding screen and lots of green crepe paper covered with trees in white chalk. As the dormouse, Gary curled up inside an enormous papier-mache shiny brown teapot with a washing up bowl base. Colin was the Mad Hatter with a top hat; Paula was the Queen and the Duchess; one of the Matthews children was the Cheshire Cat and another was the White Rabbit. Wearing a billowing 1950s party dress that belonged to my sister, I played Alice. We made giant playing cards, crowns, bugles and everyone supported us in our revival of an earlier school tradition. Later we tackled Snow White although by then, doubling was necessary to cover all the parts. Again, the play took shape with much support from family and friends. Much inspiration came from my sister, Ruth, who was already committed to working in professional theatre and heading for Drama College. Enormous woolly hats were knitted for the dwarves; fake jewellery was made for the Wicked Queen as well as an evil looking apple. Who came and how we performed I cannot recall but it was great fun.

Looking back, The Hollies gave me a great deal. The individualised teaching helped me to read after a slow and interrupted start. A fascination in history, geography, theatre and the natural world remain with me and the wish to climb trees and dig holes hasn't completely gone. The Hollies also linked a disparate family together as it was one tangible thing we all had in common. The school always seemed to be there, even though I knew it had been in different places, too. Like the Aga where we put wet clothes to dry, it was a comfortable place to be, slightly out of this world with its canteen of silver cutlery, huge paintings by my great grandfather, ancient bison horns and a Chinese cabinet full of tiny drawers. Despite the rows of coat pegs, and the upstairs schoolroom painted a lurid green, it was a house and a home with a school in it. The pyramid shaped paper milk cartons with their blue tags and the wearing of the grey school uniform were some of the few links to other schools. In most ways, going to the Hollies was something unique. I think I sensed some of that as I travelled each day. I know I sensed it on the day I took my eleven plus at another school big enough to be an examination centre. I definitely knew it on the day it closed. I can still picture the school inspector slowly coming down the stairs holding his briefcase on an afternoon in late July 1968. It was indeed a year of change.

CHAPTER 12

The doors of the Hollies Private School had finally closed, bringing to an end fifty-three years of one family's dedication to passing on the knowledge and values of a previous generation. In their different ways they tried to keep pace with the changing world around them, often with considerable success although scientific discoveries or new theories presented Phyllis Bird with ideas which conflicted with her personal religious beliefs. She never lost her fascination for Science, an interest no doubt fostered by the long hours she and her brother Francis had spent with their father when he poured over his vast collection of microscopic slides, something the younger children did not experience.

My mother Jeanie's interest in history and travel would ultimately influence her decision to leave Light Oaks. Retirement after such a hectic working life was difficult. At one time, both she and my aunt considered sharing a suitable property with me in Poole where they could maintain their independence. It was a time when the housing market was slow and I could not sell my house in order to buy the larger property. Had I been able to do so their retirement years and indeed my own future would have been very different.

Some months later, my sister and her husband suggested that they moved to a house in Surrey that they were buying for their own retirement. They had work related accommodation so did not need it for their own use. It seemed a good idea to my mother. Nora was a doctor. She and her husband enjoyed European travel and Jeanie invariably accompanied them during school holidays helping to look after her grandchildren.

Phyllis had considerable reservations about the proposed move. Although she had agreed to move to the Dorset coast where I had my home, she knew the area well from pre-war holidays. She now realised that she did not want to leave the Bagnall Parish. Francis who had died in 1965 was buried at St Chad's, his memorial a joint tribute to their parents who had been so closely linked with the church. Annis and Arthur and the child Oswald had been buried in Hartshill cemetery.

Phyllis's foster daughter and family lived in Stoke-on-Trent, and while Jeanie went to Europe, she was accustomed to sharing Jean's annual holiday.

The bond between the two elderly sisters had strengthened with the passage of time, particularly since their elder brother's death and the mysterious disappearance overseas of their younger brother Lionel nearly two decades earlier. Phyllis finally agreed to move, having been assured that she would have a garden at the new house and would be able to take her own holidays when and where she pleased. It was a sad day for us all when the Hollies and Moorside, which had meant so much to so many, were sold. Nonetheless, on my last visit when I saw Phyllis and Jeanie together, I was touched by their protective care of each other, a heart-warming memory of two wonderful old ladies. Phyllis passed away in 1981 and Jeanie in 1985, both being laid to rest in a parish graveyard so far away.

Four generations of Jeanie's descendants are scattered around the world, as are many of the former Hollies' pupils and their progeny. It appears that among them the influence of that great school family founded almost ninety years ago is remembered with affection. Annis Bird, my grandmother and the school's founder, was a quiet modest but determined Victorian lady. She would have considered pride a sin, but one can feel proud of what she and her daughters achieved, a legacy that still lives on.

There appears now to be no records in the local archives which relate to the school. One can only suppose that any folder which had existed, was not deemed of sufficient importance to be retained when the educational files of the Staffordshire area were relocated.

Fond memories of the School, however, remain in the hearts of many a former pupil, the privileged gift of being educated at the Hollies, a mainstay in numerous lives.

Index